The Karma Yoga

Chandan Sengupta

ISBN 978-93-5559-238-5
© Chandan Sengupta 2021
Published in India 2021 by Pencil

A brand of

One Point Six Technologies Pvt. Ltd.
123, Building J2, Shram Seva Premises,
Wadala Truck Terminal, Wadala (E)
Mumbai 400037, Maharashtra, INDIA
E connect@thepencilapp.com
W www.thepencilapp.com

Author biography

Author is working in the field of Science, Technology and Informatics since 1995 onwards.

CONTENTS

Karma Yoga

Yoga stands for a way of living that often satisfies a person through exposing the individual to its supreme master and the related divine. It also links an individual with all such forces which can play a defining role on the way of experiencing the Divine omnipresence.

There exists different literary and ritual sources having enough potential to correlate the human practices and related philosophical beliefs. We cannot simply deny the existence of any supreme power only on the ground of its non-visibility. In some cases such supreme power may remain off the limit of our senses. If we try to sum up all such teachings duly proposed by thinkers and philosophers of olden times, then the collected instructions will become enriched one. It will address all sorts of propositions and concern related to various aspects of our daily life.

Most interpreted literature among all is Bhagvadgita. Different saints considered it differently and also tried to work out its relevance in our daily life. Relevance of the teachings of Gita has an everlasting impression in the minds of thinkers and philosophers.

Most commonly discussed part of all such propositions is the considerations related to the essence of Karma Yoga (the Yoga of Performance, Actions and Perfections). We cannot translate the Sanskrit term "Karma" directly as "Actions" in English. The term Karma has a wide range of considerations. It correlates skill acquisition, mental preparedness for getting indulge in activities, establishment of correlations in between different aspects of life and remaning attached to the aspects of actions and perfections.

It is also true that we cannot segregate any living being from its external world. We can even assign a definite task for that individual on the basis of the skills and competence possessed by the same. Our expectation from that individual will be centralised on the basis of such considerations. We consider that individual successful only after ascertaining the meaningful and fruitful participation of the same in the proposed action. A knowledge base empowers an individual to define its role in society, or to work in the extended environment. It can even ascertain its own horizon of activities. That individual can even surpass trying days with the help of the organised framework of knowledge.

We acquire skills in life through series of interactions and training, gain competence through guided practices, confine ourselves to certain segments of duties and concerns as per wishes, mechanise our welfare and warfare for fulfilling individual as well as collective concerns and claim our status on the basis of our role in the community. Through all such efforts, carrying types of skill acquisition and knowledge confluence, we feel the presence of a masterly power having affinity of guiding the self. It even intends to make an individual a special one by providing scope of ascent in terms of spirituality. Spirituality of specific type and its expansion by all means is the subject where mind, body, skills and competence culminate properly to ascertain the refinement of an individual.

While talking about absolute knowledge with its super confluous characters we may feel some sort of difficulties due to limitations of our senses. We want to see some relevant things, but our senses may not equip us properly in doing so, similar the situation is regarding all other senses. Such kinds of sensuous limitations compelled us to imagine about the presence and propagation of some super natural things with extra ordinary characters. We cannot segregate matter and energy in our surrounding by any means or by any mechanism. Energy involvement is there even at the stage of certain sub atomic state of bindings. In the same way we cannot segregate the God or divine power from its creation. We can feel its presence but may not be able to describe it by furnishing evidences. We can talk upon it the way a blind person talks to another visually impaired ones, or like a physically challenged one with another person having similar limitations.

Our present effort is a continuation of all such previously organised efforts of making the divine confluous through our senses, making an individual feel its presence within the sub conscious mind. An earthen candle cannot describe its glory. It is the subject of other individuals having an opportunity of getting enlightened amidst darkness by placing oneself juxtaposed to the earthen candle with an affinity of getting illuminated. The Sun cannot describe itself by any means, it is solar radiation and the act of Nuclear Reaction taking place at the surface of the sun which describes the power game of the ignited giant. We also cannot put us in a move to reach the surface of any star to examine the mechanism duly involved in its affinity towards act of availing radiations, we can feel it and gain it with its graceful vitality to enrich ourselves.

There are many other instances available in our nature that describes vividly the presence of such divine power with its empowered vigil of creations and destructions. We can simply feel them, and in certain instances correlate them with our acts of creations and destructions. We can even make some of our efforts a prolonged one through designing participatory efforts of specific type for enlightening the phenomenon of the divine omnipresence. It is the realm where all individuals in this planet can feel the essence of exercising the global communion and can impart themselves in making the nature more confluous, more vibrant, more and more habitable and more prosperous.

Spirituality brings lives closure, makes people awakened, provides a scope of feeling the presence of divine power within the scope of living beings and intensifies our senses and makes us more contented for gaining the power of our effort of assimilating knowledge.

In this publication we limit our discussion on and around the relevance of Karma Yoga in present day context. Yoga of Action, Perfectness and Performance has a close link up with the knowledge base of a performer, because of that reason we can point out some aspects of the confluence of knowledge to enlighten the core principle of Yoga in an integrated fashion. It will be more exemplar for people to ensure its practical utility. Things already mentioned in Upanishadas were pitched in again in Madbhagvadgita to make people aware of the practical utility of acts and conducts of a Yoga based life.

A Yoga based life can have a sense of completeness for ensuring complete unfoldment of petals of skills and competences. It will even make people aware of the ongoing situation. Because of that reason also Yoga comes in the fore front of discussion time to time with a clear apprehension of individual as well as collective progress.

Our tendency to add a prefix with the term Yoga by using different terms like Karma(action, perfection, skills and competence), Jnan(knowledge), etc. All such ideals related to Yoga ultimately points out towards the accumulation of some positive waves for experiencing a link with the Divine and, at some higher states of practice, to feel the presence of such Divine in every creation. When any confluence of such positive waves come on surface through experiences and practices we cannot bifurcate them from one another. It is also a state of feeling the presence of all such waves with a band of stress on some other states of Yoga. Confluence of action, perfection or skill, for an example, without adequate support of knowledge may not be a desired result of Yoga. Here becomes the concept of Integral Yoga alive.

Author

October 2020

Preface

Any individual having an aspiration of gaining ascent in life through developing an understanding on the principles of Integral Yoga can go through it repeatedly. One time reading may be an eye opener. Language of this work is kept simple to enable a person having some basic knowledge of the language can explore the entire representation in original.

Students learning in high schools can also use it as their reference manual for developing their own understanding on the Philosophy of Yoga and Meditation. It can successfully enable them to develop their own ideas on the practical aspects of Yoga and Meditation.

Whenever we interact on yoga, a commonly discussed name usually comes in our mind, Saint Patanjali, the creator of eight fold Yoga Philosophy (Ashtanga Yoga). It has a long lasting impression on the lives of people moving across it by part or by full. It is the path through which one can purify one's mind, body and intellect. People having affinity towards Patanjali and his principles of yoga can also go through this book to ascertain oneself in the real world situation.

This yoga philosophy is also helpful for individuals having an affinity towards attainment of true knowledge which is required for reallocating the skills, competence and intellect in one's mind to facilitate proper manifestation of the individual within stipulated time frame of the cycle of life.

If our mind sanctions enough support regarding our capabilities of exploring real facts related to Yoga then all other debates related to the philosophy of Yoga will become acceptable at a single instance.

Any argument related to existence or non-existence of any supreme power can be addressed suitably through absolute knowledge that we gain in our phases of learning. We have incorporated various aspects related to yoga based life for addressing major aspects of various life forms. We also move through limits of our senses for not having capabilities of exploring things beyond the scope of our senses. Siply because of our in-capabilities, for an example, we cannot claim the non-existence of bands of energies like infra red radiation, ultraviolet radiation, magnetic forces, infra sonics and ultrasonics.

Introduction

Indian society is deeply influenced by the Vedic Culture and tradition. Different foreign invasions from Middle East and Europe have failed in diffusing the deep attachment of people with the teachings and observations of Veda, Epics and other Philosophical teachings. It has even made people capable of retaining their fundamental value system intact amidst the turmoil of foreign culture duly impregnated by westerners.

Learning even continued beyond the scope of interactive curriculum transaction with an aspirations of enhancing critical skills and confidence of the active members of the society.

In simple words, we can say that the advanced Value system enabled people to understand and maintain their fundamental value system on the basis of the popular cultural and traditional base of olden times. For widening this type of practice with an aspiration of collective progress, people started sharing minute particulars of their feelings on any specified thing or propositions to keep the progressive trend active and to ascertain its ascending mode.

The gradual refinement in value system has come in the form of rituals and observations. In modern day context the human value system has a character of an exhibit of a convergence of differently developed value systems. The kind of convergence of both eastern and the western value system has enabled the development of Missionary Culture in the Indian context. Such missionary culture has enabled people to readjust their acts and conducts on the basis of some masterly instructions that they duly received through scheduled discourses of their masterly guide. None of such value system is entirely aligned towards the west and not even towards the Vedic culture. Combination and recombination of value system always reflect some sort of Yoga Philosophy with an affinity towards naming it differently for making oneself satisfied. Lord Buddha, for a simple example, has cultivated eight fold simple path of worship having a proposition identical to that of the Yoga Philosophy and acts and conducts duly proposed by Saint Patanjali. The path proposed by Lord Buddha became popular in some of the society due to advent of easiness in the worship.

The missionary culture in Bengal duly introduced by Shri Ramakrishna has the identical affinity of bringing the Yoga based acts and conducts to people with easiness. It has also designed a service oriented mechanism of worship based on the principle of "Serving Man, Serving the Divine." It has also gained success and brought its prominence through cultivating ideals of Saint Patanjali. Ramakrishna wanted people to keep faith on the presence of the Divine. As we cannot feel the presence of all kinds of waves of energy because of our limitations of senses, similarly we cannot feel the omnipresence of the supreme power within us because of our in-capabilities of imbibing the waves of the supreme power. Only because of this reason we cannot deny the presence of such divine power within ourselves and within the others.

We can see things as they occupy a definite shape. We cannot see energy and power due to their in capabilities of occupying space. To feel the presence of such powers in our surrounding, we often take the support of our senses and feelings. In some cases our observations are evidence based, in some other cases it may have some imaginary propositions. Here comes the act of limitations that restrict us to feel Ultraviolet and Infrared radiations which remained off the band of the visible spectrum and duly restricted our sense of vision seven visible waves of light.

Once people of Kolkata wanted to judge the knowledge base of Saint Ramakrishna. A group of learned persons and veterans from the city visited the temple where Ramakrishna used to deliver his services by preying goddess Kali in his own language and also by claiming incidents of his conversation with Goddess Kali. The matter became very critical when Raasmani, the main patron of Ramakrishna, came to know about this incident. Inmates of the temple and the royal family wanted to work out any alternatives, but firmness of Ramakrishna made them more confident about the knowledge enrichment that the saint had.

People came in and took their respective seats within the small residential block of the fellow saint. His happiness and contentment exhibited his firmness and fearlessness. People prepared to throw questions towards him. With a gentle smile Ramakrishna described a narration in short, "Once an idol made of salt moved on to measure the depth and expansion of ocean. We all can easily imagine what happened to that idol. Returning back from his status became impossible. I have nothing more to say, now it's your turn. Ask me."

The kind of voice and firmness to face all sorts of questions made people worries about their own limit of knowledge. Ramakrishna had narrated an incident which was from Vedantic teachings. It made people confirmed about the knowledge enrichment of the saintly person having a common look with some uncommon adherence to the immediate divine. The judgement went on differently and some among them had accepted Ramakrishna as their true guide in their respective path of spiritual ascent.

Spirituality, in its true sense, should not put any individual off the track of society and culture. It should cultivate the essence of true knowledge for the purpose of the collective enrichment of the referred commune through making their overall spiritual ascent towards integral progress more and more confluous.

Instead of having all such knowledge of Veda, Epics and other spiritual worshipping mechanism, Ramakrishna preferred offering food to Goddess Kali in the way people offer to any other living beings. The kind of contentment itself exhibited his effort of linking people of some common living to their holy mother and immediate divine.

Most critical aspect that Saint Ramakrishna had to handle appeared in front of him in the form of Narendranath Dutta, later on popularly received the name Swami Vivekananda. Naren wanted to judge the actual claim of Ramakrishna regarding his conversation with the divine power. Repeatedly he started approaching his master and repeatedly started blaming him for his claim of enjoying divine communion as a false one. Ultimately the day came when the young Naren had something to beg during his divine communion. It was arranged by his master to nullify the doubts and confusion which was hampering the intellect of the young student of Philosophy. The conflict in the mind of Narendranath was going on due to his contradictory knowledge of Western and Eastern Philosophical ideas, due to his affinity of examining divine power with an intention of jotting down scientific evidences, due to his lack of true knowledge regarding non-avoidable coupling of matter and energy and due to his lack of faith in exploring the divine omnipresence in some incidents of immediate surrounding.

Depth and expansion of the knowledge is so enormous that we can simply feel it and try to acquire it by part on the basis of our capabilities, willingness and interests. Once people of Kolkata wanted to judge the knowledge base of Saint Ramakrishna. A group of learned persons and veterans from the city visited the temple where Ramakrishna used to deliver his services by preying goddess Kali in his own language and also by claiming incidents of his conversation with Goddess Kali. The matter became very critical when Rani Raasmani, the main patron of Ramakrishna, came to know about this incident. Inmates of the temple and the royal family wanted to work out any alternatives, but firmness of Ramakrishna made them more confident about the knowledge enrichment that the saint had.

People came in and took their respective seats within the small residential block of the fellow saint. His happiness and contentment exhibited his firmness and fearlessness. People prepared to throw questions towards him. With a gentle smile Ramakrishna described a narration in short, "Once an idol made of salt moved on to measure the depth and expansion of ocean. We all can easily imagine what happened to that idol! Returning back to his original status became impossible. I have nothing more to say, now it's your turn. Ask me whatever you want to ask."

The kind of voice and firmness to face all sorts of questions made people worries about their own limit of knowledge. Ramakrishna had narrated an incident which was from Vedantic teachings. It made people confirmed about the knowledge enrichment of the saintly person having a common look with some uncommon adherence to the immediate divine. The judgement went on differently and some among them had accepted Ramakrishna as their true guide in their respective path of spiritual ascent.

Spirituality, in its true sense, should not put any individual off the track of society and culture. It should cultivate the essence of true knowledge for the purpose of the collective enrichment of the referred commune through making their overall spiritual ascent towards integral progress more and more confluous.

Instead of having all such knowledge of Veda, Epics and other spiritual worshipping mechanism, Ramakrishna preferred offering food to Goddess Kali in the way people offer to any other living beings. The kind of contentment itself exhibited his effort of linking people of some common living to their holy mother and immediate divine.

Most critical aspect that Saint Ramakrishna had to handle appeared in front of him in the form of Narendranath Dutta, later on popularly received the name Swami Vivekananda. Naren wanted to judge the actual claim of Ramakrishna regarding his conversation with the divine power. Repeatedly he started approaching his master and repeatedly started blaming him for his claim of enjoying divine communion as a false one. Ultimately the day came when the young Naren had something to beg during his divine communion. It was arranged by his master to nullify the doubts and confusion which was hampering the intellect of the young student of Philosophy. The conflict in the mind of Narendranath was going on due to his contradictory knowledge of Western and Eastern Philosophical ideas, due to his affinity of examining divine power with an intention of jotting down scientific evidences, due to his lack of true knowledge regarding non-avoidable coupling of matter and energy and due to his lack of faith in exploring the divine omnipresence in some incidents of immediate surrounding.

1. Aspects of Integration

Teachings of Veda and Epics are from age old traditins. After the Epic Age we have passed on a span of thousands of years. Are such age old teachings becoming irrelevant day by day? Is the discussion on such teachings becoming useless in present day context?

If we start searching proper answer to these questions then we have to rely on the fact of the exact relationshsip with which the time and philosophy move on.

Actually Philosophy and Religion never take the support of the confluence of time. Time can even repeat itself through predetermined actions. Philossophy never intends to influence the normal cycle of the confluence of time. Therefore, both of these aspects of our daily life are independent of each other and reflect themselves independently.

What happened in Epic Age and the way Lord Rama handled the situation during that time had a deeper impact in the society during that time. It has exhibited the value system with which a State and a family can define their role in society. Those values are still relevant. Advent of any change in the material world has no power of influencing the fundamental value system with which a community leader should work.

There are millions of books and narratives with some noble initiative available for explaining and elaborating the propositions of teachings of Gita. Gita is relevant for both learners and teachers. It has something to say even to a layman having less knowledge about the mysteries hidden amidst the conversations displayed in the holy book of Gita.

The term Gita directly links our thinking with the conversation that took place in between Arjuna, a Warrior from the side of Pandavas, and his friendly guide Krishna. It was going on amidst a critical situation in which Arjuna lost his power of finalising something justifiable to have a sanction of war and killings. A series of killing of such type in which his beloved ones were at a threshold. Krishna took the role of his charioteer to normalise the situation and to let Arjuna understand his own status in a better way. The agitation, as described in the holy book of Mahabharata, was against the stand of his own family members having intention of grabbing all the resources by taking advantage of some conspired game-fares. The game-fare of such type with in infliction of opportunistic ideals were moved on differently and both the segments of a single family took a stand against each other.

Lord Krishna defined his stand by putting himself in the side of Pandavas with a sheer commitment of not to use his weapon at any instances. It was his stand that made him free from direct indulgence of the warfare and made it possible to guard Pandavas through delivering timely relevant instruction. In this way he has secured his position similar to that of the brain in our body. Conversation of Krishna and Arjuna amidst the battle field was also an act of holy instructions duly issued for Arjuna to signify his timely need. It had linked senses with duties, established correlation between rights and duties, issued bands of things to be done and things not to be done, entangled a spirit with its higher source, conferred the juxtaposition of creation and the creator and finally re-established need of knowing the self.

Madbhagvad-Gita, as the complete term coined for the holy book, had also defined the role of divine power in infusing values within the intellect and senses of a fellow devotee. It has also established a perfect correlation between knowledge and devotion. None of the paired combination alone can succeed in bringing fame.

Through all the eighteen chapters of the holy book, Godly propositions were incorporated by saints and philosophers who has created it for commons. It has a perpetual compilation of various combinations of practical aspects of Yoga and Meditation. It has also narrated the true nature of Knowledge that often receive a confluence more confluous than that of a stream. Attainment of such knowledge is a subject of individual apprehension and resides solely on the purity of mind.

Our discussion up to this point has made a point clear about the nature and proposition of knowledge confluence remaining evident amongst us since centuries with a clear impetus of facilitating its follower for gaining an ascent through divinity and perfectness. There exists narratives in different forms and in different languages meant primarily to make people aware of the eternal philosophical aspects related to teachings of Gita.

Another effort of making Gita simple, easy to understand, more confluous to attend aspirations of people, more perpetuated to incorporate aspirations of millions and more conferred to actualise role of senses. Efforts may be of varying kinds to satisfy aspirations of people in different ways out. It may have some more relevant narratives that can efficiently link up the need of fundamental values reflected by Gita at different instances.

Effort is also made to curtail unwanted explanations for maintaining the flow of the vibration of thought process intact. Discussion on any philosophical aspects should not go in a hurry and also it should not be too slow. It should have adequate stress of combined segments of knowledge and information to keep things enlightened and actualised.

It will be even more perfectly balanced to contingent human efforts of ascent towards the state of the unification of conscious mind with that of masterly guide. Effort is also made to encompass the segregation of individual differences from the common philosophical knowledge to make it more people friendly and more relevant, as well as time tested one.

Gita, in its actual sense, stands for some sort of compilation that people can sing. It can be discussed with some beautiful rhythmic tunes. Collective recitation of Gita brings out a collective wave in the form of auditory vibrations for the purpose of cleansing the immediate surrounding. It also conferred essence of collective and community level worship for making the entire effort possible and for keeping the converged senses of cooperation and brotherhood alive.

To a compilation of prayers and songs meant for the supreme lord the World Poet coined a term "Gitanjali" for it. To adhere the practical aspects of life and mission of an individual with the specified spiritual destiny, Saint Vinoba coined the term "Katha Gita (Gita through a series of stories)" and incorporated all the teachings and narratives of Gita in absolutely friendly way. Examples are in plenty. It had not diffused the glory of the original compilation of Gita, also had not conferred replacing the original poetic compilation with millions of narratives. Waves of vibrations that the chanting of Gita creates is based on the assimilation of collective vibrations of saintly senses that makes a way out through the surrounding of the place of worship and gives birth to an essence of keeping the collective vibrations of cooperation, brotherhood, divine omnipresence and interlinkages of senses alive.

We, in the same manner, can successfully create hundreds and thousands of such narratives duly inflicted with fundamental human values to make the spark of Gita a confluous one, a vibrant one and a strategic one. It has enormous power of accommodations for incorporating all sorts of socially and culturally relevant directives within the scope of its teaching related to individual refinement impregnated with spiritual ascent. It also makes the relationship of creator and the creation a vibrant one. We can specify any of the particular effort as an initiative inflicted with divine power meant for accomplishing certain works. All such Gita, duly compiled by saintly people, are not with us. In due course of time we have lost many of such beautiful, relevant and time tested compilations due to various reasons. Our mind kept on imbibing presence of such powers tradition by tradition through many of our rituals. Those graceful efforts played a significant role in keeping waves of community worship alive.

Gita was interpritted differently by different saints since olden times. Still we have a lot to explore from it in the true sense. The teachings and discourses duly incorporated by Saint Veda Vyasa reflects the teachings of Upanishads put together. Saint Vyasa wanted to incorporate all the fundamental value system and yoga based life in a compact compilation to provide people an ease of access to the divine knowledge.

If we correlate different scriptures and Epics side by side then the value system duly reflected through all the propositions of saints will reflect each other's presence in common. We can better understand this aspect by taking an example of idol making. We use clay for shaping it differently to reflect our imagination and art, similarly the case is there with Philosophy of Yoga. We can correlate Yoga with all aspects of our life. In that sense we can even say that, "All Life is Yoga."

This extended philosophy and belief cannot cripple our mind and intellect. We can even, for an example, consider the life of a beggar as a manifestation on the basis of Yoga. The beggar prepares the mind for begging something from any individual. In failing to get anything the fellow beggar prefers to move on further to gain a living. Ultimately the fellow beggar surrenders himself/herself at the disposal of the almighty. Time cannot permit us to move as per our own wishes and willingness ,but philosophy can do so. We can even adhare to certain principles and propositions to express our wishes and willingness to move through such doctrines.

People maintain faith on certain principles and rituals in which they feel themselves properly secured. Such security feelings will give birth to a communion having identical wishes and willingness. They even come across certain rituals to accomplish the jointly with an affinity of exhibiting a community feelings.

Devotion

Devotion, in its absolute sense is a state of mind in which the fellow devotee intends to offer all sorts of success, sorrow, gain and loss at the service of the divine master. Such a masterly guiding force makes the ascent of devotee towards a state of completeness possible. There exists different states and degrees of devotion possessing equally competent capabilities suitable for an individual to work out activities meant for fulfilling wishes of the referred master.

Not only that, a devotee can even perform actions without feeling much difficulties. Devotion is the state of mind that makes the union of knowledge, intellect, courage and will power possible. It also makes the devotee fearless by means of nullifying the doubts of success. It also nullifies the feeling of supremacy which hampers the continuous progress of an individual in the path of ascent towards the state of divinity. It also makes the individual competent enough in feeling the essence of following masterly instructions before ascertaining any action as a final one.

We come across the name "Kapidhwaj", the name coined for the chariot of warrior Arjuna. Once Arjuna met the legendary character of the Indian Epic Ramayana. It was none other than the warrior Hanumana. We may not require any introduction to explain the bravery, courage, will power and devotion that Hanumana exhibited in those days. Arjuna claimed his supremacy and knowledge of Archery a unique one and indulged in a debate with the saintly warrior of courage, will power and devotion. His claim was to prove the strength of a bridge made of arrows a strong one, even stronger than the Adam's Bridge duly constructed during the period of the invation of Sri Lanka by Rama and his group of soldiers. While demonstrating so, it was an utter failure for Arjuna. As per the previously finalised deal he had to ignite himself for sacrefising life. Arjuna indulged in such kinds of arbitrary deal with Hanumana without knowing the legendary importance and strength of the warrior and devotee of lord Rama.

Lord Krishna stopped Arjuna from sacreficing himself by claiming that there was no witness to ascertain the deal. The performance of the construction of bridge by using arrows repeated again. This time also Hanumana stepped on to it and it started collapsing. Only a new thing developed this time was some bood shed from the water sarted moving up. It was none other than the lord himself in the form of a turtle kept on holding the bridge in the middle with an intention of making Arjuna victorious. Hanumana identified his master in other form and agreed in helping them by all means.

Instead of getting directly involved in the struggle of Kurukshetra, Hanumana agreed to accompany them with a condition of having chances of gaining knowledge from his fellow master. That flag with a symbol of presence of Hanumana coined the term "Kapidhwaj" for the chariot of Arjuna and made it quite special amidst the war and turmoil of Kurukshetra. Gita was delivered there in the battle field for fulfilling the desire of Hanumana for having an opportunity of gaining knowledge.

Nine different forms of devotion was also described in the epic Ramayana, and duly exhibited the same through differnet legendary characters duly presented in it. Hanumana was at the supreme state of such devotion. His devotion to his master was not a blind one. He had a state of intellect, understanding, courage and will power. While moving towards Sri Lanka for the first time he started asking some opinion from his elders and exhibited his higher state of mental contentment. There chances came to establish a hold upon immense potential of wealth. He has pefered bypassing such opportunity and decided to move on. Instead of having enormous power of killing the demon king and bringing Sita back then and there from the captivity of the demon king, he has decided to convey the message of presence of Sita to his master first. Only devotion made him perpetually conted and kept him free from the clutch of ego, anger and boasting attitudes.

It also signifies the essence of devotion in the process of unfolding the skillful mind and making it available for being used. Such an increased horizon of intellect can surely increase the potential of a doer. It can even equip a person with aspirations of maintraining higher state of mind for establishing a perfect balance between memory and intellect. With such a balanced state of memory and intellect one can gain desired potential in stipulated time.

Divinity

Is it difficult for any ordinary person to have an experience of witnessing the holy touch of the divine master? Is divinity something special which can open up horizon for its follower after ascertaining the balanced state and enrichment of mind and intellect?

There is no such correlation between literal enrichment of mind and experiencing process of divinity. Divinity is the state of mind where people start recognising one's role in the society and all other acts and conducys of that individual are duly accorded. It cannot ascribe any state of attainment of such perfection without adhering oneself entirely in the path of worship. Divinity cannot even make a person off the trachk of society and cannot allow oneself to be entangled amidst any rituals and conducts. King Gopal Singh of Malla Dynasty once refused to fight against the Maratha invadors. The reason was that there was a ceremonial worship of Madan Mohan in the state capital. All the citizen of that state were also observing the week for worshipping their lord. Ghasker PAndit, the headman of the Maratha oppressors moved in easily and reached up to the state capital with an easy confluence. There occured the miracle. That miracle has created some argument. Bhasker Pandit and his men were smashed badly by two strange and unidentified warriors. Their bravery were the exemplar ones. Some of the fellow inmates of the state capital identified on of the warrior as none other than the Madan Mohan, the divine power of the kingdom, himself. Some other fellow thinkers lost their faith on any chance of occurance of such a miracle.

Keeping faith is , therefore with its genuine format, an individual apprehension that guides the person considerably in mantainng or rejecting any ideas and propositions. Ascent of the individual on the path of divinity is also ascertained by the state4 of mind on the ground of any intention of acceting or rejecting any ideas.

Intellect, Memory and Skill

We have two different segments in our brain meant specifically for memorising things and analysing things. Both the format of brain functions are compared and maintained perfectly with an involvement of one intermediary sensory power. Perfectly balanced mind maintais adequate balance in between memory and intellect. It is also regulated considerably by our wish factor. What we wish that we often do perfectly.

Here lies the mystery, why we have so many differences in individual apprehensuions and their understanding on the accommodation of such a supreme power within the junction of memory and intellect. On the basis of such balanced apprehension the success and failure of any individual is ascertained.

Intellect alone cannot fulfil the desire of the individual. Memory alone cannot graduate bthe effort of any individual for making efforts a fulfilled one. There should be proper and timely culmination of both memory and intellect for making the effort a successful one. Sometimes our senses move differently against our will power and , by doing so, hampers our efforts of implying adequate and timely culmination of memory with intellect. There requires a masterly guide, a way out for us having adequate capabilities of bringing success in the form of a divine ascent. It is a form of proper actualisation of our senses for making our efforts meaningful, timely relevant, graduated and human friendly. This type of effort can even intend the individual for harnessing the aspects of collective progress duly meant for some common good.

There are millions of books and narratives with some noble initiative available for explaining and elaborating the propositions of teachings of Gita. Gita is relevant for both learners and teachers. It has something to say even to a layman having less knowledge about the mysteries hidden amidst the conversations displayed in the holy book of Gita.

The term Gita directly links our thinking with the conversation that took place in between Arjun, a Warrior from the side of Pandavas, and his friendly guide Krishna. It was going on amidst a critical situation in which Arjun lost his power of finalising something justifiable to have a sanction of war and killings. A series of killing of such type in which his beloved ones were at a threshold. Krishna took the role of his charioteer to normalise the situation and to let Arjun understand his own status in a better way. The agitation, as described in the holy book of Mahabharata, was against the stand of his own family members having intention of grabbing all the resources by taking advantage of some conspired game-fares. The game-fare of such type with in infliction of opportunistic ideals were moved on differently and both the segments of a single family took a stand against each other.

Lord Krishna defined his stand by putting himself in the side of Pandavas with a sheer commitment of not to use his weapon at any instances. It was his stand that made him free from direct indulgence of the warfare and made it possible to guard Pandavas through delivering timely relevant instruction. In this way he has secured his position similar to that of the brain in our body. Conversation of Krishna and Arjun amidst the battle field was also an act of holy instructions duly issued for Arjun to signify his timely need. It had linked senses with duties, established correlation between rights and duties, issued bands of things to be done and things not to be done, entangled a spirit with its higher source, conferred the juxtaposition of creation and the creator and finally re-established need of knowing the self.

Madbhagvad-Gita, as the complete term coined for the holy book, had also defined the role of divine power in infusing values within the intellect and senses of a fellow devotee. It has also established a perfect correlation between knowledge and devotion. None of the paired combination alone can succeed in bringing fame.

Through all the eighteen chapters of the holy book, Godly propositions were incorporated by saints and philosophers who has created it for commons. It has a perpetual compilation of various combinations of practical aspects of Yoga and Meditation. It has also narrated the true nature of Knowledge that often receive a confluence more confluous than that of a stream. Attainment of such knowledge is a subject of individual apprehension and depends solely on the purity of mind. Our discussion up to this point has made a thing clear about the nature and proposition of knowledge confluence remaining evident amongst us since centuries, with a clear impetus of facilitating its follower for gaining an ascent through divinity and perfectness. There exists narratives in different forms and in different languages meant primarily to make people aware of the eternal philosophical aspects related to teachings of Gita.

Another effort of making Gita simple, easy to understand, more confluous to attend aspirations of people, more perpetuated to incorporate aspirations of millions and more conferred to actualise role of senses. Efforts may be of varying kinds to satisfy aspirations of people in different ways possible. It may have some more relevant narratives that can efficiently link up the need of fundamental values reflected by Gita at different instances.

Effort is also made to curtail unwanted explanations for maintaining the flow of the vibration of thought process intact. Discussion on any philosophical aspects should not go in a hurry and also it should not be too slow. It should have adequate stress of combined segments of knowledge and information to keep things enlightened and actualised.

We acquire skills in life through series of interactions and training, gain competence through guided practices, confine ourselves to certain segments of duties and concerns as per wishes, mechanise our welfare and warfare for fulfilling individual as well as collective concerns and claim our status on the basis of our role in the community. Through all such efforts, carrying types of skill acquisition and knowledge confluence, we feel the presence of a masterly power having affinity of guiding the self. It even intends to make an individual a special one by providing scope of ascent in terms of spirituality. Spirituality of specific type and its expansion by all means is the subject where mind, body, skills and competence culminate properly to ascertain the refinement of an individual.

While talking about absolute knowledge with its super confluous characters we may feel some sort of difficulties due to limitations of our senses. We want to see some relevant things, but our senses may not equip us properly in doing so, similar the situation is regarding all other senses. Such kinds of sensuous limitations compelled us to imagine about the presence and propagation of some super natural things with extra ordinary characters and potentials. We cannot segregate matter and energy in our surrounding by any means or by any mechanism. Energy involvement is there even at the stage of certain sub atomic state of bindings. In the same way we cannot segregate the God or divine power from its creation. We can feel its presence but may not be able to describe it by furnishing evidences. We can talk upon it the way a blind person talks to another visually impaired ones, or like a physically challenged one with another person having similar limitations.

Our present effort is a continuation of all such previously organised efforts of making the divine confluous through our senses, making an individual feel its presence within the sub conscious mind. An earthen candle cannot describe its glory. It is the subject of other individuals having an opportunity of getting enlightened amidst darkness by placing oneself juxtaposed to the earthen candle with an affinity of getting illuminated. The Sun cannot describe itself by any means, it is solar radiation and the act of Nuclear Reaction taking place at the surface of the sun which describes the power game of the ignited giant. We also cannot put us in a move to reach the surface of any star to examine the mechanism duly involved in its affinity towards act of availing radiations, we can feel it and gain it with its graceful vitality to enrich ourselves.

There are many other instances available in our nature that describes vividly the presence of such divine power with its empowered vigil of creations and destructions. We can simply feel them, and in certain instances correlate them with our acts of creations and destructions. We can even make some of our efforts a prolonged one through designing participatory efforts of specific type for enlightening the phenomenon of the divine omnipresence. It is the realm where all individuals in this planet can feel the essence of exercising the global communion and can impart themselves in making the nature more confluous, more vibrant, more and more habitable and more prosperous.

Spirituality brings lives closure, makes people awakened, provides a scope of feeling the presence of divine power within the extent of living beings and intensifies our senses and makes us more contented for enabling us in gaining the power of our effort of assimilating knowledge.

2. Conflicting Intellect

It will be even more perfectly balanced to contingent human efforts of ascent towards the state of the unification of conscious mind with that of masterly guide. Effort is also made to encompass the segregation of individual differences from the common philosophical knowledge to make it more people friendly and more relevant, as well as time tested one.

Gita, as a common and popularly contemplated term, indicates towards a subject related to the holy book of Gita having bands of knowledge in the form of a conversation in between Arjun and Krishna. This reality made Gita confined to a limited quarter and placed other holy efforts underneath a shadow of ignorance. We rarely talk about Ram Gita, Sanskaar Gita and some other such efforts having a suffix Gita attached to it.

 Gita, in its actual sense, stands for some sort of compilation that people can sing. It can be discussed with some beautiful rhythmic tunes. Collective recitation of Gita brings out a collective wave in the form of auditory vibrations for the purpose of cleansing the immediate surrounding. It also conferred essence of collective and community level worship for making the entire effort possible and for keeping the converged senses of cooperation and brotherhood alive.

To a compilation of prayers and songs meant for the supreme lord the World Poet coined a term "Gitanjali" for it. To adhere the practical aspects of life and mission of an individual with the specified spiritual destiny, Saint Vinoba coined the term "Katha[1] Gita (Gita through a series of stories)" and incorporated all the teachings and narratives of Gita in absolutely friendly way. Examples are in plenty. It had not diffused the glory of the original compilation of Gita, also had not conferred replacing the original poetic compilation with millions of narratives. Waves of vibrations that the chanting of Gita creates is based on the assimilation of collective vibrations of saintly senses that makes a way out through the surrounding of the place of worship and gives birth to an essence of keeping the collective vibrations of cooperation, brotherhood, divine omnipresence and interlinkages of senses alive.

We, in the same manner, can successfully create hundreds and thousands of such narratives duly inflicted with fundamental human values to make the spark of Gita a confluous one, a vibrant one and a strategic one. It has enormous power of accommodations for incorporating all sorts of socially and culturally relevant directives within the scope of its teaching related to individual refinement impregnated with spiritual ascent. It also makes the relationship of creator and the creation a vibrant one. We can specify any of the particular effort as an initiative inflicted with divine power meant for accomplishing certain works. All such Gita, duly compiled by saintly people, are not with us. In due course of time we have lost many of such beautiful, relevant and time tested compilations due to various reasons. Our mind kept on imbibing presence of such powers tradition by tradition through many of our rituals. Those graceful efforts played a significant role in keeping waves of community worship alive.

Wider diemnsions and expanded coverage of the teachings of Gita often make people worried about what to follow and what not to follow in real life. Also in some cases it becomes difficult to think about propositions in the actual ground. Because of lack of timely relevant practical knowledge of the situation, people even keep themselves aside from following and internalising teachings of the holy book in the real life situation. Approach of such religious and cultural teaching, therefore, should have proper considerations of some practical aspects of rituals and worships.

Some people maintain a view regarding Gita is that the entire aspects depicted in this holy book is a confusing one. Saints from olden times worked differently to show that Gita is much relevant in terms of rituals and propositions presented in it. Here also we are trying to traceout a link up in between rituals, traditions and practices that we have in nature to re-establish the age old faiths of the omnipresence of divine within us at its varying formats.

We can see things as they occupy a definite shape. We cannot see energy and power due to their in capabilities of occupying space. To feel the presence of such powers in our surrounding, we often take the support of our senses and feelings. In some cases our observations are evidence based, in some other cases it may have some imaginary propositions. Here comes the act of limitations that restrict us to feel Ultraviolet and Infrared [2]radiations which remained off the band of the visible spectrum and duly restricted our sense of vision seven visible waves of light.

A State of Mind

Is it difficult for any ordinary person to have an experience of witnessing the holy touch of the divine master? Is divinity something special which can open up horizon for its follower after ascertaining the balanced state and enrichment of mind and intellect?

There is no such correlation between literal enrichment of mind and experiencing process of divinity. Divinity is the state of mind where people start recognising one's role in the society and all other acts and conducys of that individual are duly accorded. It cannot ascribe any state of attainment of such perfection without adhering oneself entirely in the path of worship. Divinity cannot even make a person off the trachk of society and cannot allow oneself to be entangled amidst any rituals and conducts. King Gopal Singh of Malla Dynasty once refused to fight against the Maratha invadors. The reason was that there was a ceremonial worship of Madan Mohan in the state capital. All the citizen of that state were also observing the week for worshipping their lord. Bhasker Pandit, the headman of the Maratha oppressors moved in easily and reached up to the state capital with an easy confluence. There occured the miracle, which has created some argument. Bhasker Pandit and his men were smashed badly by two strange and unidentified warriors. Their bravery were the exemplar ones. Some of the fellow inmates of the state capital identified one of the warrior as none other than the Madan Mohan, the divine power of the kingdom, himself. Some other fellow thinkers lost their faith on any chance of occurance of such a miracle.

Keeping faith is, therefore, with its genuine format, an individual apprehension that guides the person considerably in mantainng or rejecting any ideas and propositions. Ascent of the individual on the path of divinity is also ascertained by the state of mind on the ground of any intention of acceting or rejecting any ideas.

We have two different segments in our brain meant specifically for memorising things and analysing things. Both the format of brain functions are compared and maintained perfectly with an involvement of one intermediary sensory power. Perfectly balanced mind maintais adequate balance in between memory and intellect. It is also regulated considerably by our wish factor. What we wish that we often do perfectly.

Here lies the mystery, why we have so many differences in individual characteristics and their understanding on the accommodation of such a supreme power within the junction of memory and intellect. On the basis of such balanced apprehension the success and failure of any individual is ascertained.

Intellect alone cannot fulfil the desire of the individual. Memory alone cannot confer the effort of any individual for making all initiatives a fulfilled one. There should be proper and timely culmination of both memory and intellect for making the effort a successful one. Sometimes our senses move differently against our will power and , by doing so, hampers our efforts of implying adequate and timely culmination of memory with intellect.

There requires a masterly guide, a way out for us having adequate capabilities of bringing success in the form of a divine ascent. It is a form of proper actualisation of our senses for making our efforts meaningful, timely relevant, graduated and human friendly. This type of effort can even intend the individual for harnessing the aspects of collective progress duly meant for some common good.

A mechanism of superconscious mind and its interaction with divine moves through culmination of knowledge, skill and intellect with an apprehension of gaining some sort of spiritual ascent. That spiritual power is the ultimate guide of an individual which acquires adequate power of redefining the mission of a life.

Gita , on the one side, intends to bring forward those essential propositions people should make oneself acquainted with. It also aspires for integrating all principles of Yoga in a true adherable format for making the soul enlightened. Such an enlightened spirit is the doorstep where the individual identifies the hidden mystery related to the inwardly embedded divine power. After such an identification one can reallocate spheres of rights and duies for ensuring the asent of the individual on the path of spirituality.

Exhibits of a proper coordination of rights and duties in our surrounding can be explained differently by pointing out different incidents from our surrounding. Once there was a saintly person from Bengal. He was in a wandering state and was moving from place to place to ascertain the real reason of problems and agony that the motherland was moving through during that time. During one of such turn of his visit, he was in a remote village of Gujarat. There the santly person delivered lectures. People even approached him for discussiong some common personal problems. Gradually all the fellows left the place where the arrangement of night halt for the saint was duly made by villagers. Amidst the dim light of the earthen candle saint recognised that one person was still waiting there in the room. Perhaps the person might be in trouble! May be, due to some critical problem, he wants to discuss with the master alone! Whatever be the case, saintly person approached the fellow villager, "It's too late my dear brother! You are waiting here for anything?"

With jointed hands and respectful eyes, the fellow farmer came closure to the saint and said, "All people went away. You had lots of interaction with many people. Now what about your dinner, my master?"

Situation was entirely different. The farmer was not worried because of his any individual level or family level problems. It was his worry about the hospitality of the saint. He was much worried about well being of the saint. The duty delivered by him during that time has melted the ego of the saint for his state of a claim regarding his much religious, much spiritual and much awakened status. The kind of quality exhibited by the farmer in practical way was a lesson for the saint. It was a lesson for him in a way of enabling him to consider every soul in this universe a potent divine nucleus. A powerful mind filled with knowledge can ascribe the exhibit of such noble conducts.

Actually the farmer was from an untouchable community and was feared of being trapped by villagers while offering food to a saintly person. But, the saint wanted him to feel he joy of offering cooked food to a saint; a state of pure and selfless sacrifice. It was a kind of lesson for the saint to have an opportunity of witnessing the manifestation of divine conduct in an ordinary farmer. He had exhibited his spiritual supremacy over the saint by fulfilling his timely need.

After noticing the incident all the fellow villagers greeted the poor farmer for his readiness in performing his duties and for his effort of making the master pleased. The kind of readiness, empathy and courage exhibited by the fellow farmer was also implied an impression in the mind of that saintly person and played a vital role in diffusing the sense of some masterly feeling which was at the stage of some primordial growth.

A devotee should have adequate knowledge of the context and of the propositions duly delivered by his fellow master. The person should be capable enough in maintaining transposition of such waves of thinking in maintaining the vibrant relationship of fellow master and concerned follower. A devotee should have adequate understanding of sequencing instructions properly and delivering the same whenever need arises.

Devotion without knowledge is just an act of bodily function without any active involvement of brain. It may rarely make a person competent in keeping, maintaining and delivering instructions and propositions as per need. Even some of the acts of the individual may remain emotion driven. A true deevotee with adequate knowledge can accompany the fellow master during accomplishment of some planned tasks. Such a balanced mind can even impart several intellectual guidances and intends to retain waves of knowledge as of a normal confluence.

Once a devotee was watching his master doing some critical meditation meant for individual advancement. That fellow approached his master with an aspiration of learning the same mechanism of individual advancement. It made his master little bit unhappy. Actually the fellow master wanted his follower to acquire qualities of a shady tree like that of Banyan. Such a conduct can give shelter to hundreds of others. Aspiration of adhering and working for personal advancement like that of a palm tree is absolutely useless affair. Observing the wishes of master the fellow disciple has changed his mind and preferred preparing himself for the service of humanity through cultivation of community progress and community worship.

Here developed the idea of collective and community level worship. Through such worship a society can successfully accommodate aspirations of collective progress perpetually for ascertaining the development of all. At the stage, when people started maintaining different ways and means of worshipping their supreme master, we put adequate emphasis on the ways and means of ascribing community level unity for an aspiration of making participant community more successful, more vibrant, more confluous and perpetually aclamatised for diffusing community level tensions. Community level worship and related mechanisms developed differently during pre-independent scenario in India. That time it was the necessity for bringing people together and preparing them both physically and mentally to fight the brute forces. Modification also advanced in the Ashram system of living and collective worship duly meant for cultivating a convergence of ideals and rituals.

Gita implies stress on the advancement at both community and individual level for enabling the probable transfusion of fundamental human values in society. First condition for obtaining success at this juncture is devotion to a system. But such devotion should have proper understanding. Once all inmates of an Ashram instructed a youth to accept his master without indulging in any argument. But the youth was not ready to go on such a way. He had a clear apprehension of examining the excellence of his master regarding spiritual enrichment, then only the fellow can be accepted as a true master. He went on examining his master repeatedly for diffusing all his doubts before acccepring the saint as his master. Such kind of approach exhibits a devotion with clear understanding of one's role in society.

Repeated examination of the fellow master incarnated him towards attainment of perfectness in worshipping the Divine. There he came to know about the language with which one can talk to the Divine Almighty. It is actually the state of mind from which any disciple can correlate a conversation with the supreme power and a perpetuated guide. That was the state where the dialect of the masterly mind was relying on to the acquired ones. In that sense the act of the fellow disciple to come out of the state of confusion through examining the masterly mind was also a justified one. There was no trace of any absurdity.

3. Knowledge Confluence

Shopkeepers worship their beloved God before opening the hut, industrious people worship God just before cementing the first brick of their construction works, crafts person worship their instruments during some fixed interval of days to commemorate the supreme power. Worship of energy and efforts is the custom of universal occurrence. There occurs an emotional attachment of artisans with their instruments. They even take care of their instruments on a regular basis. Gradually they come up with an enhanced vision of putting their efforts to keep all the instruments at perfectly operational state. They even consider their instruments as their immediate focus of scheduled daily activities.

Nobody claim the direct interaction with God, but we can feel the presence of such divine power within ourselves. Manifestation of such power will put us at a state of success, where we become fearless in delivering our best possible efforts and services to our immediate reference group. That state of awakening will be the accomplishable goal for any individual including the fellow artisan.

The nature and extent of support, not only in the form of technical knowhow but also in the form of assistance to cope up with market, should be considered for making the system implement appropriate for the rural artisans and farmers. More perpetually one can plan to link up the community with the immediate availability of the resource base for ensuring greater chance of success. Proper combination of Resource, Technology and Skills can define the scope of attaining success. Development workers, since olden times through varying approaches, always worked to search out proper technology, proper mechanism to rely upon, living within minimum, and also moving out of the activities leading toward creation of best possible products and services. They also marked out the fact that technology to be adopted should be people friendly and easy to handle, even it should be compatible to the type of resource base a community relying upon. All sorts of absurdity should be removed.

Lack of confidence upon the system and its implements is the immediate set back that often brings the entire chain of productivity under question mark. One rarely prefers to wait up to the moment of the creation of any enhanced demand of the locally developed products. Better one should launch the implements on an experimental basis duly supplemented with a subtle increase in the productivity.

Financial Institutions always imply a prolonged processing of any appeal of fund. It should be made flexible in terms of availing ease of access to small and marginalised artisans. There is other side responsible for the complexity of the processing of any appeal of finance. Most of aspirants become defaulter while moving across newly implemented enterprise leading toward a severe loss because of the mismatch of resource, technology and knowledge. Yoga based actions never pass on with any blunt apprehension of such failure ultimately leading towards any mis adjustment between resources, skills and technologies. Mis-adjustment of resources, skills and technologies often becomes so worse in some cases that can even put a crafts person or farmer to a life risk. Situation of farmers in Vidarbha because of indebtedness can be placed as an example.

Here we can take an example to exhibit the lack of proper coordination between the planning and implementing agencies duly involved in some development works. One such incident was recorded from the same area of Jharkhand during 1995. Some fellow farmers of Nimdih Block of Saraykela District of Jharkhand received Bullocks financed by a Nationalised Bank. Loss of the life of one of the bullock made another one useless, and in a gradual succession the farmer trapped in the clutch of the financial crisis because of the lack of any immediate return in terms of productivity. The marginalised farmer again trapped in the net of turmoil because of the intervention of a private source of finance for clearing the Bank Loan. The Bank was not in a situation to bring the farmer out of the previous indebtedness because of the rigidity of the financial regulations of the Development Initiatives of the government.

While planning for any industrial activity suitable for a specific rural community, one can imply the credibility of the selected products as per the global standards. Standards of such level can bring the entire system to a stream of implements having more focus upon the look and finish of the outcome to be entangled with the market system. Product should say its own purity and perfectness. It should even attend and apprehend the quality consciousness of people willing to rely upon the same. It should not even break the linkages of demand and supply for enhancing the systematized permanence. This kind of market mechanism will undoubtedly increase the market demand of the selected item.

If any business house of Europe implies stress upon manufacturing Artificial Fabrics with greater success indicators, the same can be housed in the National Economy with higher index of success supplemented with profit. Productivity should go on parallel to the demand that duly created in market. One should remain stick to the mechanism after considering the global demand. Competition alone cannot define any effort as a fruitful and time tested one. One should work to correlate acquired skills and competence of fellow workers with that of the technology available to us. Here arises the need of implementing a discussion on true knowledge.

Veda, Upanishad and other scriptures of Indian origin always describes true knowledge as a subtle confluence of streams of information and skills having adequate power of abolishing the cultural blindness and spiritual rigidness through bringing transformation in characters and will power. Knowledge is the only thing that grows on sharing. It never shrinks to its minimum. A tree of knowledge, as described by saints in Gita, spreads its leaves downwardly in the form of Vedic teachings. The upwardly spreading roots of prosperity receive continuously confluent source of knowledge from the divine and nourishes the entire creation through millions of exhibits of such knowledge. Theory of Relativity, for an example, was not there waiting in the chamber of the fellow scientist. It was there in the cultivation of his skills and ideas which, with an ultimate manifestation, enabled him to link up his observations duly required for deriving the theory. His deeper involvement in that specified faculty enabled him to weave such linkages of theries and propositions.

We always witness the manifestation of such supreme knowledge through its creations. It can even imply a guiding force for all the creature residing in the immediate surrounding. Such a prosperous sacred fig tree (Peepal) can bring forth the absolute knowledge in the form of a normal and continuous confluence of waves of thought processes. Veda described it as an eternal one. It has a sequential expansion having a parallel pace of such considerations through knowledge transformation. Keeping oneself free from illusions and selfishness, one can realise the true nature of absolute knowledge and accordingly can put efforts to gain such kmowledge at its absolute nature for making oneself contented and complete.

Down flow of senses and sensible actions become materialised through passage of such waves from the divine to the disciple with an active involvement of masterly minds. This confluence of knowledge and related mechanisms properly explained in chapter fifteen of Gita. One can get rid off the confluence of such relationships of manifestation by cutting the linkages of willingness and desire by using weapons of absolute knowledge. Desires[3] amd wishes in the form of leaves grow downwardly growing tree and gains further enrichment through addition of more concepts and propositions by saints. The hidden core of all such knowledge resides only in the absolute confluence of pure knowledge through roots.

If one start moving from leaves and move gradually towards rootlets, then the enlightenment come in the form of repeated crystallization and refinement of knowledge in a regular progression. The final destiny in this way will be Divine only. Involvement of such power in all sorts of creations and actions become critical at that moment. In actual sense the source and the destiny of the confluence of energy experiences a linkage between various aspects of manifestation. Naormal confluence of energy throough the cycles of creation and destruction are absolutely inseparable ones. A Black Hole, for example at this critical juncture, is the seat of destruction and creation. From one side all mattrs and manifestations winded up for accelerating the pace of reversely directed streams and waves of creation.

This absulte knowledge empowers us adequately and facilitates us vividly during our process of identifying presence of divine in every individual with an absolute state of our contentment. Gita even facilitates us in the process of our understanding of the evolutionary trend remaining evident in the biosphere.

We can take the example of the experiences gained by a saint namely Madhavdasji [4]during his wandering days in holy places. The saint was with an absolute state of devotion and used to collect remaining food left out by sainly persons of Ashrams. From such a collection he used to offer it to the Divine first. It was his daily routine activity. One day he was late in moving out for collecting such residues from ashrams and because of a forgetfulness he had taken a few without offering it to the Divine. After taking the food in mouth he has realized his mistake and started weeping like a child. He went on weeping in the same posture and the food remined in his mouth.

He was in a dilemma of his inability of taking any concrete step. He cannot take that food witout offering it to his lord, even he could not spit it out for insulting saints who had offered him that food. With such a simplicity and comtentment he had an experience of feeling the presence of his master within himself only.

Madhavdasji experienced presence of Divine power near him and got an instruction offering the same food that was there in his mouth. Such a call was even firm and absolute for conferring the presence of similar power within himself. It was directing him to forget about physically evident differences. This state of mind developed in Madhavdasji because of his absolute contentment and faith on the source. He has sacrificed all his wishes worries for incorporating the impulse of Divine in the form of absolute impulse of thinking and action. His actions has correlation with mind and intellect and his intellect was developing on the basis of his repeated actions and meditations.

4. The Limit of Our Senses

We are discussing at present about saints like Veda Vyasa, Maharshi Patanjali, Valmiki and many more. There presence can be ascertained even today through their creations, acts and conducts. They had created a best possible thought process and expected people to imbibe the same for ensuring aspirations of the advancement of the society through rectifications of the individual conducts.

Rectification of such type is a continuous process. We may not be able to claim about the absolute clarity on the process of rectification as an error free system. Such kinds of thout process will remain in the atmosphere even after thousands of years for making people acquainted with such principles.

The kind of thought process will remain in the context in the form of waves. Now a days wave theory of the propagation of energy from its origin to the seat of action has become a common point of discussion. Wave theory of the propagation of energy form place to place addresses the need of people well in advance.

Thinking and attitude of people coming out from more or less identical socio-cultural background often exhibit similarities of many types. If countries from different socio-cultural background share parts of their border then it will be obvious that they often get indulge in some locally pitched conflicts. We can take the examples of the conflict between Armenia and Azar Bizan. Some other countries also put themselves in with certain vested interests. Communities fighting with each other is not justifiable at any cost. There exists other means of communication through which people move on to express their anger and also they can imply a sanction through business confluences.

Here comes the question of work culture and sectoral coordination. We have also witnessed the attitudinal difference between Rama and Ravana, as vividly described at difference instances in the famous epic the Ramayana. Rama wanted Ravana to give Sita, his life partner, back. He had deputed his messenger twice for making Ravana, the demon king from Sri Lanka, agree upon the proposal of peace.

The proposal of peace was rejected in one hand and the power, potential and courage of lord Rama was ignored on the other. The result came in the form of a war. That war was also not meant for killing all the people of that country. It was not even meant for smashing the kingdom for grabbing resources, nor even meant for putting the name and reverence of lord Rama in the fore front. It was meant for teaching a lesson to the demaon king and also for diffusing his state of ego, compulsion and desires.

The thought process that started moving along with the advancement of lord Rama was perfectly captured and imbibed by the brother of the demon king namely Bibhishan. He had managed himself to come out of the darkness of ego, compulsion and desires by harnessing the philosophy of peace, prosperity and collective progress. The result with him was also quite fruitful. He was the victorious person of that battle and duly accepted the place of his elder brother.

The Ramayana. The Mahabharata and other such scriptures always display the victory of good forces over the evil ones through inculcating waves of peace, prosperity, brotherhood, collective progress and prosperity for all. These acts also intnsefied at some places by linking up the bands of true and absolute knowledge with devotion to bring forth the powers of right action.

Hanumana, the warrior of lord Rama as described in the Ramayana, is the best example of such character having perfect combination of Knowledge and devotion. Once the situation developed in the middle of the journey of the envoy of Lord Rama when they had to cross a long stretch of ocean to reach Srilanka for obtaining information about Sita. All fellows present in the envoy started guessing about their own potentioal, only the person silent was Hanumana. His seniors wanted to know the exact reason of his silence. Hanumana said that the power possessed by him is obviously enormous, but it is not in his hand. A divine force guides the manifestation of that power. It will be implemented even at the service of the divine. Such knowledge was the exhibit of the true knowledge. Based on that knowledge one can surpass all possible obstacle whichever might come on the way. Similar thing happened with Hanumana. By crossing all the obstacles he reached the destiny and traced out Sita.

Sita noticed the presence of the messenger deputed by lord Rama. Here came the situation where Hanumana exhibited his devotion. For gaining the confidence of Sita on worriors and associates of Rama he had exhibited his enormous power in that garden where Sita was kept under observation. He even wanted to bring Sita back to Rama immediately. He was stopped by Sita by instructing him not to violate the rule of the family and tradition from which Ram is taking the lead. He was requested to follow the assignment in particular for which Rama deputed him.

Here both Sita and Hanumana exhibited there devotion to their immediate master. It was also an exhibit of their loyalty to their master. Such loyalty often culminates to give birth to enormous power with which lord Rama along with his entire envoy was advancing towards the Demon King to teach him a lesson.

The fact was developing beyond the imagination that is why it was not perceivable by persons having inflictions of ego, anger, hatred, self centerliness and desires. Ravana perceived the deevelpment in the envoy of Rama and his advancement towards his kingdom as an impossible task. After noticing the presence of Hanumana in front of him he was not convinced by the powers of monkeys and other associates who were accompanying lord Rama. The waves of devotion of the god whom Ravana worshipping was radiating out through the acts, conducts and attitudes of Hanumana. Then also Ravana was not in a position to accept any chance of the advancement of lord Rama towards his territory. Such standpoint of a warrior develops from the over confidence of the person about the system, implements and parts of such implements.

That over-confidencs removes all possible chances of rectification of the system. Because of that reason also Ravana failed to rectify his mistakes and placed himself in the turmoil of trouble.

Whatever lessons we learn from experiences and interactions will sustain in our life for a longer time period. It can even bring sustaining happiness and contentment within ourselves. Here lies the way in which any thought proess perpetually moven from one individual to the other.

In the modern world we have various types of cultural and religious thought process possessing rituals, customs and traditions of different types , which are equally competent to enrich people in terms of knowledge, deotion, courage, will power and dedication. The way we receive each culture to enrich our multiplurality will specify our degrees and ranges of success. Our motive force will guide accordingly to explore possibilities of working out a converged cultural segments from all the rituals to move up towards a vibrant waves of multi plurality.

India , at this juncture of the development of multiplurality, will be a best example for all of us. Here people learned a lot to live wih each other, tolerate each other and enrich eah other differently.

We cannot see light. Even we cannot see the propagation of sound through the material medium. Light strikes our eye, reaches our brain and develops a sensation of vision through certain life process of vision. With some sort of illusion, or lack of true knowledge only, we often claim that we can see light. Even all the colours radiated out from the sun are not recognisable by us. If God resides inside the individual, if all mysteries related to the ascent of a person on the path of divinity, then why any devotee search it out for gaining the blessings of any Divine power located outside the physically existing body? Why such a dwindling situation any individual face during the tenure of worship?

Lord Krishna narrated essence of feeling the Divine communion with the physically existing life through witnessing cultivation of knowledeg, actualisation of the presence of any supreme power in sub conscious mind and possible ways and means to follow that power. It enables an individual to come across the feeling of the advent of some completeness in the mind through knowledge transformation. Cultivation of knowledge regarding the relationship of the divine and disciple is enrouted from the age old traditions through the turmoils of the organic evolution. That evolution brought some change in the process of exhibits, but the core remained the same. It was even more perpetual and more profound regarding the ability of harneshing the relationship of matter and energy. We cannot imagin the existence of matter without the involvement of energy, and similarly energy takes a definite visible form to occupy certain space in this universe.

How do people see things and how do they correlate such unavoidable relationship of energy and matter is depend upon the level of understanding that one adhares with. A master of Physics and a master of Phylosophy must have varying degree of explanations for putting forth the mystery behind the mechanism involved during inter-conversion of matter and energy. All organic combinations has certain physical and chemical sets of combinations in such a definite ways that they inculcate the abilities of interactions and abilities of giving birth to senses. Even evolution of sensory structures and related orientations became much collaborative in case of human beings. Here occurs a change which brought us near the state of explorations meant for examining the hidden mysteries behind creation and orientation of life forms in the living planet.

These days, things are known to us that earth like situation exists in the universe. Only the matter of concern is that we may not be able to reach the place even after attaining the speed as that of light in a year or two. Only we can admire the the presence and orientation of such creations within our visibility. Only we can explore and examine such things with the help of optical and electronic instruments. With an understanding of such limitations human beings never arranged any voyage to explore the inner world of senses that can allow us to explore the outer orientation of time and space. Such an inner world exploration may require a little effort to culminate senses within a confinement for feeling the presence. There also resides a tremendous flux of energy accumulated within such a small space. That mysterious combination taking the form of life were explored differently by saints during olden times.

There developed a science of explorations of the correlations of the Creation and the Divine. Matter and energy indulged in a perfect orientation for letting senses flow through them. Arrangement and orientation of all our senses are directed outwardly. That is why we are bound to receive waves and sparks from the outside world. Our inner world remain unexplored in most of the cases. Only adherence of true knowledge and the journey of senses through inner world during meditation can pave a way out for exploring our own self. Meditation is the doorstep where orientation of senses get diverted towards the inner world and bring out mysteries associated to the fact of accommodation of the Divine power inside the living being.

Is that Divine power is restricted to the human beings only? The answer is, obviously and surely without any doubt, No. human beings has gained some sort of evolutionary supremacy in due course of time.but other beings are also of same potential and curage with a domination of animism in them. Dogs are loyal to their master, cats exhibit better vigilance power, elephants are more socialised beings having better memory power and tigers are the masters of their own territory. Taking hold upon the surrounding and defining the role according to trophic [5] level, we can easily arrange these beings and others without any difficulty.

Philosophical and Spiritual supremacy is a step forward that makes a distinction between other animals and human beings. Then also we can witness inhuman acts from human beings and humanly acts from some inhuman animals. The orientation of sense organ and correlation of senses and sensory responses with memory and intellect is the only factor regulating such varying degrees and conducts of animismic and hunmanismic behaviours.

Presence of such a Divine power within the creation is the reason behind the maintenance of an idea of serving humanity with a correlated apprehension of serving God. Only God cannot put a direct access to the feelings of the presence of such immense power within us. It is the approach with which we offer our services to living beings can develop a way out for us to feel the difference.

Once a youth from Mumbai approached a saint for offering himself at the service to divine. It made the saint happy. He wanted to know the exact reason behind his stand of doing so. Saint also enquired about his capabilities and considered his offering a wise one. Actually the fellow was searching jobs in the city. He was also a normal Graduate from any sub –urban area and his financial situation was also not so good. Perhaps the sacrifice might make him temporarily happy and contented, but will become a burden in due course of time. With happiness saint suggested him for searching out a suitable job and helping the parents and inmates of the family financially. After gaining some wealth and knowledge only the person can really enjoy the glory of sacrifice. Right now the person has nothing special to sacrifice. Such sacrifice inflicted with sorrow and agony may put both the master and the disciple in trouble.

Even divine cannot allow any individual to put oneself and families in trouble and agony. It is the only state of contentment that helps a person during movement from the physical world to the spiritual world. Offerings of any kind and in any particular form will bring happiness.

Once a shopkeeper had a beautiful dream. The dream was so beautiful and so perfectly understandable that he feared of sharing it with others. According to his dream the God himself wanted to visit his shop. It was winter season and more special about the time that, it was raining outside. Amidst such patchy rains he preferred opening the shop. Inmates were knowing it better about his firmness upon any decision. He prepared some sweet dishes, some snacks and few cakes for the strange visitor of the day. Face of God was appeared in dream and was not recognisable with any clear identification marks. "The Master must introduce himself, or may give some signal so that his poor fellow can recognise", his happiness went on increasing bit by bit.

"Can I have some snacks and a cake?" An old lady was approaching the shop with a can on her hand.

"Today, actually I've not opened the shop! If you came then please, have it."

"Guest! Some special or any usual one!" Curiocity of the old lady alarmed the shopkeeper for keeping the matter a secret one.

A cowboy was approaching holding a fruit in his right hand. "That guard is chasing me. Let me come in, please."

"But, you are already inside my shop! Anyway let me see the fellow.."

Cowboy narrated the entire incident behind the reason of his hunger. That fruit was kept aside and the shopkeeper offered him a dish full of sweets, snacks and cakes.

"Don't worry my child, I'm here with you."

The matter settled in an hour. The noon time bell of the cathedral instructd the shopkeeper to finish his meal. But, what about that strange visitor! There were no traces of such visit amidst the sprinkling of droplets in the courtyard and a shower on the roads.

Evening time visitors were a cobbler, a masson, a hawker and a vagabond. Earning was not the matter of the day that is why he offered food to all the visitors with respect. It became possible because of his happiness. At last the mind refused to support him properly. Entire day and half of the night went on waiting for the master. Ultimately the time came to stop waiting for the strange visitor. His mind was still in a motive of receining the visitor. May be the master is trying to meet him when calmness mounts the surrounding. With such anticipation he preferred keeping the door half open.

"So nice! So sweet! Really all items were tasty.." , the masterly voice brought his happiness back in dream.

"I may visit you again and again."

Morning time dream mixed up profusely with chirping of birds and silver linings of the clouds.

"God came! Who was that? May be that boy! .. " Series of anticipations and guessings went on for few moments. The entire face of the shop keeper was glistening with happiness. It was the time for feeling the presence of the Master in any nearby position. It had developed a faith in his mind, "My Master must come and visit me again."

We cannot deny the role of a school in the life of any individual. The person gains a lot during school days. S(he) can learn how to impart oneself in the society by redefining ones role in society.

It is not the only aspect of life through which any individual gets an opportunity to expose oneself to the fundamental value system prevalent in society. One's choice factor plays a definitive role in this regard.

Cultural background of an individual is greatly influenced by the immediate surrounding. Human beings, for an example of an ordinary type, is vegetarian by nature, but omnivorous by intended vigil of gaining some essential proteins from the animal sources. Development of canine indicates the biologically and naturally assigned habit to human beings. If we aspire for remaining confined within the naturally sanctioned habits of our own then the acts and conducts related to the killing of animals for the shake of gaining essentials will definitely go at its minimum.

Killing of animals for obtaining food and medicine is perpetually inflicted with acts of animism. It also signifies the place of human beings at a definite trophic level. It has also exposed our relationship with other organisms and our dependency upon the source. We rarely make ourselves capable of trpping waves directly from the sun. It will always reach us through the involvement of producers (such as green plants). Maintaining green plants in nature and allowing them to prosper in our surrounding is, therefore, becoming a non avoidable activity of the system in which we are confirming our presence. The referred system also limits our ascent and conducts. Within that limit of acts and conducts any human being can explore possibilities of registering the presence of oneself by performing the duties duly assigned to the individual perfectly, perpetually and vividly.

Escapism

One cannot escape from oneself without performing duties duly assigned by the system desgned for ensuring ineractions of different trphic levels. If we start claiming that tigers should no be allowed to kill deers, cats should not chase rats, snakes should not feed on frogs and owls should not puncture ripe fruits then our such claims will violate the laws of nature. With certain natural insticts, and for maintaining a proper balance in nature organisms ensure their definite role as per the assignments. Human beings are playing a role with some sort of exceptions. One can intend to kill deers for obtaining food, one can trap fishes, kill birds, smash snakes and chase bulls for fulfilling the need of grabbing food. With a modified vigil of registering one's presence in the cycle of energy transfer one can cultivate grains, harvest fruits and maintain mulching animals for fulfilling the requirement of food. For rest of the world the role of that human will be of a protector.

With such dual principles human beings can register the presence of oneself in between the highest and middle order of the trophic level. In another aspect we people maintain our differene from others due to our dactility, capabilities to speak, performance of exhibiting our emotions and affinity of remaining linked with others. Here comes the essence of socialisation and acculturation for the same. On the basis of such involvement in the society parents cannot escape from their duties of nourishing their children, young ones cannot escape from their duties toward eldors and seniors cannot escape from their affinity of helping young ones.

Escapism of any type and any degree is the affinity of human beings for which the entire community may face sufferings, loss of trust and agony. Escapism of any type can also create individual differences, depending upon which human beings often start ascertaining one's role in society.

We cannot claim that all people make themselves capable enough to esxape from the acts of escapism and make themselves more active, more responsible, perfectly awakened and properly adjusted.

5. Standard of Living

Sometimes we claim that people living in some cultured civilisation lead a higher standard of living. For all instances of life process they are more equipped and more perpetuated than compared some other people belonging to sub human standard of living.

Objection regarding the Standardisation of living in terms of mechanisation of life process is not the only scale depending upon which one can classify different society and different culture. Standard is the relative term with some limitations of its own. People involved in the process of standardising a society or a person may consider some parameters on the basis of the knowledge base that the person possess. Differences in the observation will be observed on the basis of the knowledge base of people involved in such mechanism.

Every individual in this society differ from the other at any of the points. There may remain more differences or may remain any one difference. It may be in terms of capabilities, it may be in terms of skills or may be in terms of competence.

On the basis of such formats of differences none of the individuals in this world are of useless type. Everybody has a definite role to play here. We can correlate attitude of any individual with those of some olden times in terms of similarities and differences. Such comparison is of less importance because of the reality that every individual is of its own type. Then question arises, how do people encompass some similarities in attitudes and conducts with those of some characters remained prevalent in olden times? Is it true that Lord Rama can take birth again? If yes, how?

Similarities and differences that we come across is due to the system of socialisation and cultural blend that people come across during the process of acculturation. A child, for an example, rarely agrees to sit alongside other fellow students during early days of schooling. It is more prominent if we try to isolate a child from their parents. The kind of mental adjustment is developed on the basis of faith that grows inside the mind of the fellow learner.

Learning of any type, at this crtical juncture should not be a forced one. It should not try to suppress the individual identity by imposing any unbalanced curriculum having no adjustment with the immediate context. Epics like Ramayana, Mahabharata and holy book like Gita became evident only because of the ease that these scriptures and allied literature provided for accelerating the pace of learning. Another such famous creation that gained adequate attention of people is Ramcharitmanas written by Goswami Tulsidasa. People found their intellect more adjusted with the narratives of Goswami Tulsidasa.

When we talk about the philosophy of peace, it points out toward doctrines of certain fundamental human aspirations in which the human mind attains a constructive status. Peace never stands simply for diffusing anger, tension or any other unrest. It is not the exhibit of any termination of tension or war. It cannot be considered as a dogma opposite to violence, unrest, struggle or fighting. In its absolute sense, peace is a part of the yoga based life duly proposed by Vedic saints as a state of mind. It even ascribes the entire human effort to reestablish that state of peace in the immediate surrounding, and finally in the entire world. It can be stated that Veda describes the attainment of utter calmness and establishment of harmony in the world as an exhibit of peace. Peace is the only state of dwellings in which one can cultivate the possibilities of practicing all sorts of cooperation, brotherhood leading the entire creation finally toward harmony.

Ahimsa is often referred as nonviolence in English. But the term, nonviolence is not reflecting the absolute nature of the term ahimsa as the absolute form duly projected through theories of yoga in Vedic Philosophy. Special emphasis of elaborating the term ahimsa is implied in the works of Patanjali, Buddha, Mahaveera and in a more practical way through the life of Mahatma Gandhi. Still then, we accept the term and replace ahimsa by the negative aspect of violence that often stretch out the meaning of the term nonviolence for accommodating some of the absolute aspects of the philosophy of ahimsa. The term ahimsa took its first appearance in the Vedantic Philosophical theories and doctrines. Patanjali considered ahimsa as one of the prominent part of the eight part yoga philosophy (Astanga Yoga Darshan) . Ahimsa was accommodated under the yama part of the Yoga theory. Without truth and nonviolence, one cannot make oneself fit for moving across the yoga practices duly reflected by Patanjali.

Ahimsa alone can make a situation suitable for all the organisms staying within certain confinement and facilitating in casting off all sorts of minute differences such as caste, colour, creed, customs etc. Patanjali described the philosophy of ahimsa by coining a simple theory of the concept that reflects the entire beauty of the inherent dogma. According to his theory, "Where nonviolence is established in its absolute sense, organisms living within that surrounding will cast off their individual differences and start leading a life like that of a single family." People living under such confinement of philosophical convergence even forget their all sorts of individual differences of caste, creed and colour.

Philosophy of nonviolence even secured its prominent position in Buddhism, Jainism and other schools of religion duly developed and practiced in the Indian context. Mahaveera delivered his doctrines of practicing nonviolence at its absolute level to be followed by Jain Saints. Buddha perpetuated his teachings by placing peace and nonviolence in the central position and instructed fellow followers not to move towards the impulse of violence for putting oneself and the community in trouble. Not to think about creating harm to any individual or to any system even in dream was the absolute doctrine delivered by saints like Buddha and Mahaveera. Most remarkable feature of such ahimsa is the convergence of culture, tradition and rituals towards attaining a communal harmony through sacrificing individually apprehended wants for the facilitation of community welfare. Balancing the need and want is another practical aspect of ahimsa or nonviolence that leads an individual toward attaining satisfaction.

Attainment of such satisfaction, in turn, will make the individual stable by mind, intellect, deed and creed. A follower of peace and nonviolence with such attainment of satisfaction and stability can ascend toward a state of self-regulated individual having adequate faith upon the self. Here becomes the union of both external as well as internal power of the individual.

Collective Worship

Worshipping God for individual satisfaction will be a matter of absurdity because of the involvement of a living being with the immediate surrounding with other fellow aspirants. Remaining away from the habitat and moving apart from the community are rarely possible for any socially awakened being in the actual sense. It is a collective worship duly ascribed for the collective progress that brings more fruitful result for all the individuals engaged in the process of worshipping God. Gandhi emphasised on the importance of regular community prayer for imbibing the benefits of collective worship amongst ashram inmates. It can even remove individual differences, diffuse caste feelings, neglect religious imbalances and promotes harmony through acknowledging the regional variations of worshipping the common Almighty.

Collective worship avails adequate facility to all individuals for exploring possible accommodation of people of all kinds of social as well as economic backgrounds. The Community of Ark duly established by Lanza Del Vasto (1901-1981) in France worked out different aspects of collective worship gradually aiming toward establishing peace and harmony within the community. Each person at the Ark works according to their capabilities and receive as per their needs. In that way none of the community members kept away from the stream of social as well as economic activities duly planned by the community. It will even enhance the self-esteem of the contributor and performer that often paves a path of continuous ascent towards individual refinement in acts and conducts. Such mechanism of collective progress is the real beauty of the life based on peace and nonviolence. The Ark can also be described as a community movement aimed toward accomplishing the common good.

What we want from Nature is enormous compared to what we offer to it in return. At least not to distort the normal situation of the immediate surrounding will be a desired inititiative. What we demand is obviously a state allowing ourselves to expose the greed up to the extreme and make our wants a voluminous one. But, our needs are the specifications of our life process that we surpass on a daily basis. We can limit our wants by regulating our greed and by establishing a subtle control upon our demands. Here our will power can help us a lot. Ultimately will power is the master regulator of our deeds and greeds.

We can even minimize our need by making our life process a simple one. Regarding this aspect Dr. J. C. Kumarappa pointed out about the prevailing confusion that often strikes the minds of people regarding standard of living and standard of life. Standardisation of any life process depends upon the type of the habitat and not on the type of self-ascribed choice. We take food as per the basic requirements of our body and not to fulfill the ever increasing greed of bodily pleasure. Kumarappa looks upon the lifestyle of Mahatma Gandhi as an example of simple living and that of any city dweller as an example of a complicated lifestyle. Achieving the goal of simplicity in life should be an ideal pursued by any individual looking for an alternative lifestyle.

Community of Ark emphasized on the necessity of manual labour, fulfillment of basic needs, simple living, embracing voluntary simplicity in daily life, adequate participation of people by consensus decision making and collective worship through community prayers. It is not the only an aspect of the collective life, but also a part of their aspirations in bringing out certain common resolutions which paves the way for the welfare of the community .

The Internal Peace

Peace and prosperity that are exhibited in real life practices is of certain vitality and can sustain for a limited time in the life process. But the peaceful state of mind duly followed by attainment of true knowledge can sustain for a longer time. It is capable enough in cultivating some noble standards of community living which in turn results in making everlasting impact of peace and prosperity in the fellow community. It can even guide the entire group towards adopting community worship for aspiring the collective progress.

Affinity of people towards attainment of collective progress exhibits a higher state of consciousness that can easily accommodate the aspirations of all the individuals leading the community life. During the practice of community worship, a state of mind comes that help us in withdrawing our senses from the external stimulations and help us in passing across the feelings of the internal spiritual power. At this juncture, we feel the presence of divine within ourselves. That almighty guides us, ultimately, to trace out the goal of our life from the ever sustaining turmoil that prevailing in the natural world.

The people who join the Community of Ark consider their goal of life as establishing peace and nonviolence or leading a life on the basis of Gandhian principles which would ultimately change the entire world for leading a peaceful community living impregnated with prosperity, courage, will power and skill acquisition. An ideal social as well as economic order of living aimed finally towards bringing all people at the base of a core competence that enables them to accept community level productive works and they become capable enough in sharing community level activities with eternal happiness of mind. The kinds of practices bring them close to feel the aspirations of fellow workers and they can refine their skills and competence through certain participatory interactive phases of experience based learning.

A broader spectrum of the implements of a community living on the bases of principles of peace and nonviolence is awaiting sanctions of various economic houses and power seeker organisations. It came up with certain collective verdicts of imposing sanctions upon smaller segments of the world where a gambling between commitments and implements is in progress since the birth of the United Nations. Sustainable Development Goals of United Nations coined various aspects of implements in its resolutions. Resolutions are to be adopted by the member nations for bringing forth the opportunity of development for all. First and the foremost threat this goal should face will be in the form of power gambling initiated by Nations and community seeking Nuclear Power. It is also an example of the diverting science and technology towards mechanizing warfare. If any joint concern appears for tackling the threat of terrorism and violence, then there should be unanimity amongst implementing agencies for ascribing the guarantee of peace and justice to common people living in the world.

Loss of the balance of the forest biota, rapid progression of urban settlements for destroying natural habitations of birds and animals, hunting , poaching and cross border terrorism are another aspect of set back towards achieving the Sustainable Development Goals because of the lack of any direct control upon people working as master minds in the kind of oppressions. Because of the strategic location, India is facing such problem since independence. Knowledge base of people involved in such conduct is not ready to move across the process of dialogue and peaceful resolutions. Diffusion of such terrorism is possible only when any peaceful resolution fits in the minds of terror seeking people and they give up their hatred.

Highly Nuclear powered nations like USA and Russia came under the process of START treaty for agreeing upon the further reduction in their power potentials duly aimed towards destructions. Such kind of initiatives will be welcomed to initiate an effort of establishing peace and harmony in a broader spectrum. There are other instruments of tackling the terrorism and brute forces of the world through imposing series of sanctions duly resolved with the concern of member nations. If the START (reduction and limitations of Strategic Nuclear

Arms) stops in the middle without highlighting adequate success in bringing the disarmament in reality, then all brute forces again entangle with shelter of some of the nations or of any specified community. A proper touch of development, access to resources and opportunity to work can diffuse the prevalence of the tension of terrorism and violence throughout the world. Human apprehensions always imply priority upon self-ascribed wants and never upon the collective needs. It is another aspect responsible for the prevalence of interpersonal conflicts and unrest.

What communities do during prevalence of any tension or unrest? Whom the communities approach during the phases of turmoil? What are the actions that we often depend upon states to consider for? Up to what extent the judiciary and law protect us from external threat and oppression and safeguard our aspirations? The answer is only one. If we compete in exercising our effort to impart ourselves in the decision making and law making process, then the Statehood and Nationhood will be a suffice in protecting our aspirations and safeguarding our development initiatives. We know that one can kill an individual, but killing any community is not the subject of violence, oppression, terrorism or brute forces. Community of Ark has set aside such example of an empowered people exercising their duties and rights with great vigil, will power and enthusiasm. Their belongingness to nature, their affinity of taking care of farm animals and exploring all sorts of trophic levels of the naturally implanted energy pyramid has paved a path towards visualising a strategy of balanced economic activities meant for the purpose of establishing a harmonmious progress within the operational area of a community. They have also marked an impression upon living within a minimum. Day by day need based planning has taken the place of greed based economic activities.

Gita teaches us life propositions, rituals and traditions in a balanced way through conversation between the warrior and his master. The master took the role of friend for an objective of minimising differences. It was also a balanced discussion with an acknowledgement of the existence of such a form of teaching from age old times.

Here developes a process to cultivate an approach in which all the Yoga practices should have a definite accommodation in the day to day practices of a physical mind and body. It should have adequate access to socially and culturally active group for making them aware of the need of community level worships, and to have an access to spiritual ascent. Such ascent will definitely sustain for a long time because of its assimilation through different segments of the society. It will also come across with a balanced and vibrant practice modulations for allowing people to develop and accept practices as per need, and also as per willingness.

From any theoretical perspectives there may exist any demarcation line between Yoga of Knowledge and Yoga of Action. But in reality, there rarely exists any sharp distinction in between such practices having a prefix Yoga. It has some common confluence with collective practices having involvement of knowledge, action, rituals, traditions and faiths. All these processes cannot be compartmentalised and also cannot be assigned differently to any individual. One can only maintain the idea of existence of such practices in reality. Integration is also unavoidable because of the confluence of waves of thought processes through identical channels of senses, memory and intellect.

We can simply apprehend the existence of such kinds of Yoga in the individually confluous practices and propostions of Yoga based actions. Knowledge plays a vital role at this critical juncture by issueing a base on which faiths, yogic practices, concepts and propositions stands perfectly. That is why success of a character can be quantified perfectly on the basis of the degree of culmination of knowledge and action at all instances of life. We can also design a tradition and practice for making our effort of integration more confluous, more vibrant and more result oriented. Gita enables us to move through such actions and traditions with an ease of understanding and faith.

There develops problem when one loses faith on the divine and adhares certain alignment towards some proposed practices simply because it was proposed by his fellow master. Such blind practices may develop problems related to the process meant for establishing adequate balance in the mind and intellect. What to do, were to do and when to do, accordingly, will become a critical aspect in life.

One can rarely claim that the utility of Gita in daily life is of negligible importance. We often remain ignorant of any of our actions to confer the role of Gita in our daily life. The reason is that, some of the concepts and rules displayed in Gita is followed by all of us without knowing the exact format of it. In this way Gita is becoming the breathing of life. If we move on through the refinement process of our actions by surfing it in the light of the Divine power then attainment of success will become a confluous one. With such confluous actions we gradually move towards attainment of completeness by all means. Gita also helps us to diffuse our ego, crush our agony and negativate our state of discontentment. It also highlights the essence of Yoga in our daily life.

Gita also establishes a view that Yoga besed life is the absolute state of life that can gain competence of feeling the confluence of absolute knowledge through transformation of mind and intellect. Integral approach of Yoga should have enough scope of nullifying all negative forces for enabling the development of personality.

A Yoga based living and spiritually oriented approaches of daily living can bring back vitality in life. Due to lack of proper understanding regarding any activity or correlations human beings often mislead oneself through getting inflicted with some sort of falsehood in life. It also maked the individual discontented. Such discontentment and lack of faith on any ritual generates a wave of agony in mind. Such a mind often fails in maintaining adequate balance between memory and intellect. It also imposes waves of such discontentment upon senses. Such imposition of discontentment upon senses surely bring falsehood in life.

Sense organs are the only enemy of human intellect and are available for being guided differently on the basis of certain prevalent pleasure principles. It can also mechanise the individual for following the sensory guidance of gaining joy. Joy is the exhibit of our attainment of pleasure. Happiness is the state of mind that states the completeness and contentment of the spiritual horizon of the intellect. We, being an individual along with our knowledge, make ourselves available for masterly instructions and expect something superior as a masterly guiding force. What we want to see that only will become visible. Similar principle is applied on all the senses working towards the centralisation of feelings for infusing the role of the centrally located dogmatic divine. That divine, in turn and by remaining unconditional, implies a guiding force upon senses for materialising the refinement process of manifestation of the invidual through acts and conducts.

Superimposition of any instruction upon the acts and conducts of any individual cannot bring fruitful result because of the lack of proper culmination between sensory responses, memory and intellect. Here lies the principle of the convergence of Yoga of different realms for making the individual a complete one by all means.

States of Inetegration

Yoga is the state of communion of the divine master and the studious disciple meant for feeling the state of communion through acts and conducts. Yoga might make the communion of the individual with Knowledge (Jnan Yoga), with actions (Karma Yoga) or with sacrifices (Sanyasa Yoga). Such communion of various types may not invade the individual senses differently. Their senses and condcuts works on the individual jointly. These different realms of acts and conducts internally make any one of them with a bit prominence upon the others.

We can understand this phenomenon with an incident from the Ramayana, where Lord Rama wanted his brothe Laxmana to behave like a true learner having enough affinity to gain knowledge, even from any sworn enemy. After the completion of the battle of Sri Lanka, when both the fellow brother came to know about the state of the final breathe of demon King Ravana, Lord Rama instructed his fellow brother to move closure to Ravana with an aspiration of learning something from the demon King.

Laxmana moved on to obey the instructions of his brother only. There was no true affinity towards the divine knowledge developed in him. Then also he was considering the demon King as his sworn enemy. Such a state of discontentment forced him to take the position beside the head side part of the demon King, the place where one can rarely glance with a bit comfort. They remained silent for a long time. During another move with such approach of learning something pure from the demon King, Lord Rama positioned himself in such a way that the fellow King can see him with an ease. It made the King convinced perpetually and compelled him to deliver a timely relevant lessons infiltrated with his life time experience. It was the learning for a politically motivated individual. Lord Rama wanted his brother to listen the teaching of Ravana with proper attention and respect. His stand and approach was to make his fellow brother a learned one. Here the mechanism of integral Yoga worked perfectly for making them aware of the state of mind duly required for any individual for gaining aspirations and timely relevant instructions from a sworn enemy.

Ravana pointed out the difference between both the fellow brothers regarding their abilities of utilising senses, memory and intellects for materialising their political and social will. Wish factors arranged properly with an intention of materialising the common good made Lord Rama special amongst the group of warriors. It has also made him perpetually contented because of the proper culmination of Yoga based acts and conducts.

Integration of senses with a clear understanding of the timely relevant acts and conducts is also a subject of the culmination of different Yoga. It is the seat of philosophy, meant for individual and a collective ascent, where the referred individual can actualise oneself through a clear correlation with the centrally active Divine. Integral Yoga [6] can even make the individual perpetually clear regarding the role in further manifestation of the self actualised power of mind and intellect.

Saints intended to converge these philosophical ideals through conversation of the divine and individual duly displayed in the Gita. Integration of individual with Yoga is the core of the principle materialised in Gita with an aspiration of enabling a doer of actions in attainment of completeness by all means. The presentation of such conversation has also exhibited the existence of such Yoga philosophy from olden times in the universe. It has evolved differently in due course of time and also narrated differently by saints time to time. Gita was, obviously without any doubt, a successful efforts amongst all of them.

Eight fold Yoga

Credit goes to saint Patanjali[7] for the development of a most scientifically acyualised Yoga conduct meant for the advancement of individual followed by a collateral advancement of the socity and of the commune. His proposal is even perpetually designed for accommodating different aspects of a noble life process duly meant for experiencing a feelings of collective ascent through the paths of spirituality.

The journey begins with a proposition of following rules of Yama (a set of acts meant for individual purity). It proposes that a person having aspiration of moving through the Octagonal path of Yoga should be nonviolent, truthful, altruistic, self contented and worshipper of knowledge. While explaining the core philosophy of Nonviolence, the saint proposed the state of mind that considers all the other beings as a family member can claim that the individual is experiencing a true state of nonviolent life.

The second fold in this life comes in the form of some rituals for gaining purity and perfectness of organs and senses. There lies the importance of cleanliness, contentment, self study, sacrifices and worships of the divine. It will simultaneously purify both the mind and body for making the individual and the referred community fit for the ascent up to the third state of this Yoga conduct.

Third stage is meant primarily for balancing the body, mind and intellect through positioning oneself in some proposed postures, termed popularly in Indian Philosophy as Asana, and regularising the same through day to day routine works. While describing such positioning, the saint says that the kind of position which offers a stability of mind, body and intellect is the Asana in its true sense. Whatever may be the posture and watever may be the name for such posture, true Asana can only bring desired stability of mind and body.

Fourth stage of the Ascent is vital one because of its involvement in diverting senses towards the inner conscious mind through regulation of the breathing and confluence of senses through specified neural transmission. The core philosophy ascribes the establishment of a hold on the breathing and bringing it down at least below 15 per minute. It is also designed for channalising the breathing through different nerve channels for infusing senses in the deep conscious mind for making it awakened and contented. This process is most vital one because of its importance in making the individual capable of diverting senses towards the inner world for roaming around the acquired knowledge and rearranging such acquisitions by repeatedly meditating on them. It can be also described as a process of self actualisation and self contentment. Such a contentment only can enable a person to move through the inner world of senses and knowledge. It can be more confluent because of its mild infiltration through all the senses. It can make a person see what the mind wants to see, it can listen in accord to the inner sense, and even taste, smell and touch things accordingly.

Development of positive waves in mind because of the proplonged meditation, the individual makes oneself fit for experiencing the practice of withdrawal from the external world for enabling oneself perpetually confined upon the attained knowledge and quantify oneself for further attainment of true knowledge. Such a withdrawal (PRATYAHARA) makes the person competent for making oneself refined and more perpetual for the ascent of the soul a step ahead for the attainment of a feeling related to the presence of the divine in the life process. It can even imply a guiding force for the individual duly required for rearranging the abslute knowledge for the purpose of making it more vibrant, more confluent and more actualised.

All the five stage practice brings a state of enlightemment for the individual and kmake the person fit for feeling the true meaning of life, real goal of life and all sorts of lively involvements in the community and ulmately , in a broader sense, in the universe. Such an actualisation (DHARANA) makes the person fir for meditating upon the stand point repeatedly with an aspiration of bringing refinement. Movement and journey of any person through this stage depends entirely upon the degree and expansion of the knowledge duly acquired by the person in life. It can ascertain the attainment of such a state of mind at the stage where senses, memory and intellect culminate perpetually with an apprehension of spiritual ascent.

Sensual, intellectual, spiritual and social convergence mounted voluntarily in an individual brings a state where the conscious mind intends to mediatate repeatedly. This state of Concentration (DHYANA) enables a person to feel the presence of such a divine power in so many different states of individual and different life forms of all types moving around in nature. Their purpose of survival, their inter dependence and other hidden mysteries start becoming clear during concentrating upon the related process and propositions. A warrior, for example, can concentrate properly at the specified target. Such a perpetual concentration can bring further refinement in senses, memory and intellest with an objective of making them more actualised, more contented and more balanced.

Fixing mind, intellect and senses upon the true attainable goal in life is the final stage (SMADHI) where the person can feel the presence of Divine in the centrally actualised Memoery, intellect and senses. It will become a guiding force for the individual and make the person competent for gaining spiritual advancement in life. It will even make the life a meaningful and perpetually contented. It is the desired stage of life where person aspires to ascend through practices, acts and conducts. At all instances it is not necessary that all people should move through all the eight folds of Yoga. The state of mental and spiritual contentment or a state of saturation aspiring for mental stability will exhibit the advent of Samadhi.

We cannot claim that individuals impartimg oneself in society for delivering services or for playing some other definite role are perfect by all means. They work ceaselessly in due course of time for attaining perfectness in a gradual succession. Some people may consider an individual as perfect as compared to some other. One player may be considered a best one in his or her team. In gradual succession best ones will be identified through a tournaments and some other best ones may be compared globally to select the globally best one. But, what about that skilful player who had decided not to take part in any tournament? The kind of act exhibits the limitation of the evaluation process as a whole.

The comparative process of examining and assessing perfectness parameter is standing on the basis of certain directives usually made by a group of people. Because of that reason any perfectness parameter cannot claim that individuals moving through the screening of the perfectness examinations are absolutely perfect. We can work put billions of questions from any specific field of study. Moving through such a massive task might make the life of any aspirant a hell. The type of testing in the form of written interaction is usually made limited by incorporating a set of planned interactions and content areas with a pre – planned format of study.

Aspirations of Perfectness

We cannot claim that our all acts and conducts are perfect. We can simply claim that we all try our best to attain completeness in our life through making ourleves more and more actualised through processes, as we feel, fit for us. It will bring a kind of perfectness. The claim of any individual regarding the state of perfectness depends upon the state of knowledge that the person gained through practices. Perfectness of one individual from any specified viewpoint might be of different type as per the understanding of some other individual. Such a difference in terms of observation and actualisation makes the term perfectness a relative one.

With relative consensus perfectness can be of relatively advanced one or may be of degraded one. That is why we feel that all individuals should have an apprehension of refining oneself repeatedly keepimg pace with refinements and actualisations in the field of knowledge acquisition.

A management school of Japan once started claiming that the management model duly designed and implemented by them is a model residing on the Zero Defect System. In due course of time that management model was replaced by the term Quality. The name coined for that management system was Total Quality Management. With further experiencing and related experimentations people came to know about the fact that the term Quality is a relative one. It has no correlation with the abslute sense of any management. Upgraded qualities of any type might have some degraded apprehensions from some other view point. That is why quality is considered as a relative term. Further advancement and actualisation in the process orientation related to operation management gave birth to a more meaningful model of management termed Total Care Management. The term Care can be actualised as per the level of knowledge and can be refined repeatedly as per need. This management model sustained in the community level activities of carrying types.

We consider the God as a perfect one and we also aspire for gaining such perfectenss with a set up of our mind for having an opportunity of feeling the presence of such completeness in our mind , intellect and senses. It will make our life meaningful through bringing actualisation of the self. It will also make us more contented through adharing all our efforts of culminating actions and propositions for a common good.

The act of Sabari [8] , as described by saints in the Ramayana, was a perfect one. The process of conducting a leading a warfare against the Demon King by Lord Rama was also a perfect one. The eleven qualities duly exhibited by Lord Shiva and identified accordingly by Gopddess Parvati were also perfect ones. They have decided to set an example through generating a legendary character, namely Hanumana (the wise monkey), for exhibiting the true culmination of Knowledge and Devotion with an objective of bringing success in all actions. Success of Hanumana was also residing in the fact of proper culmination of Knoweledge and Devotion.

Here we came, with an ease of access and understanding, at the last segment of discussion about essence of karma Yoga in life through maintaining a faith on the philosophical doctrines re established in society through proposals of Gita. It was witenssing the junction of dual battles that the person was figting just after entering the battle field. The Yoga of sorrow and discontentment as exhibited by Arjun in The Gita was the juncture where the person had to become victorius upon some inwardly active enemies. Anger, ego, discontentment, fear and some other similar enemies may put a person in trouble during the stage of a standpoint where the paerson has to fulfil all his duties, acts and conducts through exhibits of will power and courage.

Yoga of Knowledge and Action, as described with some proposed practices in Gita, always intend to bring absolute coordination between actions and intellect for making efforts a successful one. It is also proposed that the person should move on further to perform duties without wasting time by waiting for any desired results of actions to come. Such kind of adherence to result of any action may distrcat the effort of any individual and make the effort a partially accomplishable one.

Perfectnesss by all means may remain in nature, may equip a person in different ways and may configure the efforts with more prominent results. It may even make people aware by different means of progress. If one aspires individually about attainment of progress by keeping aside aspirations of other fellow partners of society, then we can say that such aspiration may never bring a reality because of the prevalence of linkages and cross linkage remaining evident in society.

Veda speaks about presence of such perfectness in God and aspires for cultivating the same by any individual through repeated and regularised practices of Yoga and Meditation.

We may continue discussion further more upon the same topic for making the fact about essence of Yoga in life a clear and prominent one. We can even represent hundreds and thousands of more examploes to highlight the essence of Yoga based life process as an ideal one. On the basis of such fact it is advanced that the effort will continue in future with an aspiration of bringing more live experiences for establishing the role of Yga based life process in making society a vibrabt one.

Progress of All

If we aspire for our own progress, with incorporating the necessity of the progress of other, then we must move on through materialising ambitious projects for ensuring progress of all the other idividuals. Progress of such type with a collective apprehension will bring success by all means. It will also make the entire community a vibrant one. People living in a community are interlinked at various instances. In a natural way we cannot sanction access to different types of water and different types of air for respective members of the community simply on the basis of their socio-economic standards.

People should enjoy thir access to resources with an easiness for ensuring their active participation in the socialisation process of the entire group. Any implements or plans meant for a specific community should have all other paraemters duly required to minimise the communication gap, information gap and cultural gap which often become the root cause of some community level tensions.

Philosophy of Karma Yoga along side the integral approaches will become the central force during consideration of any implements having scope of Progress of all the members of society.

Strategic Participation

Participation, simply meant for keeping people in confidence, while implementing any development activities, may not bring fritful result. It should have adequate scope for accommodating ambitions and wishes of maximum number of people in any planned development initiatives and work plans. One can grant a sanction upon any plan or one may directly oppose the stand of community leaders. Development wokers remaining involved in the planned actions should have adequarte explanations for gaining the confidence of people at all the levels of society.

Ignorance of any of the community member will turn into a socially developed wounds in the form of a shadow area of information and communication. Such shadow area will become the birth place of anger, hatred, tension and communal violence. There are examples in which we can see the people of oppressed classes become violent and start planning differently for exercising their rights.

If any legal and judiciary system loses confidence of people then there are chances of violations of such law at the respective level of community in which people lost their faith on the judiciary. Flexibility of the judiciary should ensure the scope of implementing any exerises for regaining confidence of people on the judiciary.

People impart in the socialised system in which they feel themselves adequately protected and properly internalised. Their rights should have adequate social and legal safeguardings. Without ganing the confidence of people we cannot expect them to catre their duties towards the society perfectly. Bhagat Singh worked and sacrificed for the freedom of India in one hand and agitated differently against Brtish on the other. Britishers wanted to smash him by putting him in the dark room and finally by sentencing him till death. Community of Indian origin started working out a strategy of violating the state law for making their leader free from the clutch of oppressors. In this way one person may simultaneously gain the status of frind to some community and enemy to the others. People may finalise ttheir stand about any community on the basis of their predetermined ambitions, wishes and willingness.

Balance of Mind and Intellect

What we speak should have adequate support of mind and what we do should have adequate support of senses. We often do things without taking much concern of our social, emotional and intellectual status. Here develops the conflict which, in a long run of our socialisation process, often hampers out emotional as well as intellectual set up. Balance of mind and intellect will be the basis of individual apprehension upon which acts and conducts of an organism duly ascertained.

People often incorporate big big ideas and ideals for ornamenting the value system for a vibrant society, but in real life they rarely follow such things. Value proposition of such types having no set up of observable things often put people in a state of duality with which they develop a conflict within the self. They can even feel what are the things better for them, but they rarely intend to blend their senses and intellect in right direction simply beause of the lack of adequate self confidence and support of mind.

Mind duly struck at such a state of duality rarely make itself capable of developing some intellectual blend and also rarely support their intellectual set up.

In modern time we all speak about humanity at different platforms of national and international characters. Such discussion often terminate with some positive resolutions of extending adequate support to the mankind. None of the organisation, in actual sense and in real life situation, can capable of implementing any initiatives for saying no to any inhuman acts and conducts. There are examples in plenty to enrich the depth and extent of the claim of such prevalence of inhuman acts and conducts at different parts of the world. People involved in such kinds of inhuman acts and conducts may give some different argument to admit their accuracy in some other context. A more intensified torture to oppose any act of torture and killing cannot solve the problem. It will burry the fire under debrices for certain time. We can expect any intensified outbreak at any time.

Diffusion of Negative Forces

Situation that hampers our individual ascent in the path of Yoga based life is the prevalence of some negative forces within ourselves. It has a deeper impact on senses. One can surpass all such forces with a commitment of imbibing positivity in all actions. By doing so one can readjust all the senses for materialising the manifestation of the spirit at all instances. With the easiness of mind this process is too easy, and with the difficulties of the mental balance one rarely capable of feeling any presence of such forces.

Self Esteem

If we start talking to a person regarding any subject matter then there will be a state of confusion in the mind of the person regarding the subject matter and related contents of the theme duly assigned to the individual. The state of confusion is only because of the prevalence of the lack of true knowledge regarding one's capabilities of doing any job with perfetness.

One can even hardly confess the difficulties that the person is facing during the proposed interaction with selected groups on any selected theme. Actualisation of any kind develops in the individual because of the presence of the Self Esteem.

Self esteem is the quality depending upon which a person organises skills and memory to prepare oneself for a right ation at right time. It has no correlation with any change that intends to bring any change in the context. Self esteem is still equally relevant in the information age. Properly organised person can materialise any action within limited resources. Even one can implement such actions with best utilisation of resources. Such kind or organised action can even bring result with an enhanced quality consideration. It can even link people with better apprehensions of collective progress.

Will Power

"What I want that I will and that I can", this general tendency of an individual makes the action a reality in actual sense. They even come forward with their willingness to impart themselves in certain activities. This will power is the centrally accommodated reason that confers the participation of people in certain activities and nonparticipation in some other.

Grouping and subgrouping of different people on the basis of caste, culture, colour and economic status is also inflicted directly or indirectly with such will powers. For making the discussion little bit clear we can consider some examples from our real life situation. Such experiences are there in plenty.

Positive Attitude

What we think in mind that we aspire to see and experience in reality. We even plan accordingly to make things happen. If we aspire for attaining success in life and duly put our plan and efforts accordingly then the desired success must come in reality.

Once emperor Ashoka, one of the powerful emperor from Maurya Dynasty during later Vedic Civilisation, invaded Kalinga[9] for punishing the culprit who was also the murderer of his mother. Kalinga was maintaining a voluminous army, even they had a democratic status. With only selected army Ashoka was more organised , confident and contented regarding attainment of success. Success was supplemented with proper planning and absolute positive attitude. That was the real mystery lying behind attainment of success by emperor Ashoka.

Hanumana, as described in the popular Epic the Ramayana, wanted to cross the extent of ocean to reach the kingdom of the Demon King with utmost confidence of attaining success. That is why his conversation with his fellow generals has reflected the type of positivity that developed in him before moving to the mission. He has instructed all his fellow warriors to wait for the information that he is going to bring from the kingdom of darkness and misery. It was that positive attitude which made him fearless during his presence in the court of the Demon King.

Designing a Strategy

Yoga speaks more about the strategy of actions that the actions or perfections. How to do any work is more important than the work itself. One can keep on drawing water from the well by using ropes and bucket, or it can be obtained by fitting a water lifting pump at the base of a pipe.

What to do, how to do and when to do are some of the pre-requisites of developing a strategy for designing a strategy. For throwing out Nanda Dynasty [10] and for replacing the same by a wise king, Vishnu Gupta, popularly known as Chanakya[11] or Koutilya in History, took the support of Greeks deputed there in Indian continent by Alexander. It was the strategy of developing friendship with the enemy's enemy. Such mechanism worked perfectly and he attained success by putting his efforts in bringing change in the Indian context. The result was a long lasting success which came in the form of good government.

Although Chanakya was the most powerful person and most respected master mind of his time, then also he preferred not to put himself on the throne. He preferred maintaining his status of a king maker.

Strategy of action and its importance was also perfectly narrated by Saint Valmiki in famous Epic The Ramayana. Once Sugreev, one of the warrior from the envoy of lord Rama, as described in the Ramayana, chased Ravana just after seeing him and recognising him through a window. It was absurdly planned and prematurely implemented. The result came in the form of a failure. Ravana managed to escape from the place by making the warrior entirely confused. He was the master of magical powers. With the help of his magical power he had handled the pre matured planning of Sugreev.

During another breefing on the need of planning for developing a strategy lord Rama narrated the need of gathering such a big army and seeking support of the brother of the Demon King for making things materialised properly within least possible casualties. Every action requires a proper planning. Winning the battle against Ravana was not so easy, also it was not impossible. Proper considerations of all aspects of threat from the demon king made Rama and his warriors more prepared, more responsive and more specific.

Even with more powerful army and different magical powers Ravana became the loser because of his poor planning, arrogance and over confidence. Adequate strategy was not worked out by him due to his act of the under estimation of the powers of lord Rama and his envoy.

Continuity and Persistane

Victory may not wait for us in the battle field and success may not come on the exam desk instantly without putting adequate efforts. We often ignore the need of proper planning for developing a concrete strategy of organising oneself for any forthcoming challenges. Because of this reason failures of different degrees and different extent put us in trouble.

It would be better if we start learning form experiences and arrange ourselves properly for any other forthcoming challenges. At this critical point the teaching of the Gita will work properly. It says that one should deserve a right to work, results will come automatically. It would be better to prepare oneself for any other forthcoming challenges without remaining fixed upon the results of any previous action. The instruction is very simple and also easy to understand. One should not stick to the result. The success might make a person full of joy and any failure may bring sorrow. Both the joy and sorrow will create bands of obstacle on the path of ascent. That obstacle supplemented with mental, physical and spiritual crippleness will put a person in a halt. Such halt may become fatal for any vibrant life form.

Planned action can bring a successive scheduled actions followed by one another in a cyclic way. Some of such planned actions often confer the consideration of some of the laws of Nature. That is why it helps in maintaining the coordination and balance of mind, intellect, skills and the body parts. Each of the parts of any individual works perfectly amidst such a balanced coordination of senses, mind, intellect and body.

Only a mind full of words, ideas and ideals cannot work properly, only a body with a strong physique can also make any action a half dome, only skill can wait for some fritful and coordinated instructions of the mind and only intellect may indulge in some sort of arguments. That is why coordinated actions of all the parts of the individual will be the only way out.

Coordinated actions will open up horizons of the possibilities of culmination of perfectly planned actions with desired state of performance. It may not wait for the results of the previous action to come. It will indulge oneself in the vibrant process of organised actions with an aspiration of feeling one's ascent through the path of spirituality and will power.

Importance of nature in our daily life is a matter beyond the questions and conflicts. For understanding such role, with a clear distinction between acts, conducts and necessity, we may go through a popular story of a beggar and King of all kings.

Once a beggar was moving through the royal path with an expectation of receiving something prosperous from the king of all kings. The poor beggar was standing by the side of a royal path with an expectation of receiving some handful of wealth. The King of all Kings often passes through that path and gives in plenty.

For making the anticipation of the poor beggar true, the band of dust with an admixture of clouds appeared at the horizon. The King of all Kings was moving in through that royal path. The very moment of prosperity and happiness would be there in the life of the fellow beggar. It might bring an end to his wandering status. It may also fulfill his desires.

The dust and cloudy appearance moved more close to the beggar and finally the moment came. A pair of empty palm were there in front of the poor beggar. The King of all Kings was begging! It made him very angry, also the act was absolutely unexpected one. With a mixture of anger and agony he had decided to offer few grains of corns to the King of all Kings.

With happiness, King of all Kings received the gift and moved on further. The day was not prosperous for the fellow beggar. His all faith and contentment on the King of all Kings duly melted. He had nothing to say but to feel, nothing to comply but to hide and nothing to offer but to gain.

Situation turned differently after returning back home. He was to sort things as per its nature and utility. Some glittering corns were of special type. His inmates identified that particular corn as costly gems. This incident made him unhappy. He understood the magical power that implied upon him by the King of all Kings. It was even more annoying to notice that the return was equally countable in terms of identical quantity of the offering. The number remained the same, but in terms of quality there was a tremendous boost. The kind of equally powered boost that he wanted to receive in life made him fully contented and compelled him to change his stand of not to offer things.

Second turn from the side of King of all Kings was about to come. This time he had prepared himself to offer his kind self at the hands of the fellow master having some sort of divine power.

He was not in a position to give up. The kind of incident made him absolutely confirmed about his stand of witnessing the magical transformation which can make him feel the action of the divine power on him. His contentment was also of absolute type because of his capabilities of witnessing the impact of such divine power on grains of corns.

Beggar symbolises a common human being bearing aspirations of progress. The King of all kings symbolises Nature. Nature is the only entity which arranges a living for all its members.

The conservation strategy is gaining a momentum. It is also widening the information gap between people and government. The schemes launched by government often remain off the record of people simply because of their non participation. Due to this reson participation of people in making the schemes successful often remain off the track. We cannot put a hold on the intrusion of unauthorised hunters and poachers in the referred area of the wild habitat. We, alone on the basis of some legal frameworks, cannot put a halt on any unlawful acts and conducts of people leading to a loss of normalcy in forest biota. We simply adopt a collaborative effort by establishing proper coordination between people, government and environment through ensuring timely participation of people in the planned efforts of the government and conservators.

From evidences available in nature, it has become clear that native Indians are not a threat to the wild population. They prefer living in a harmony as an ideal harvester of the forest resource. Their intended effort is meant simply for harvesting a living without implying any harm to the population residing there. Honey hunters of Sundarban and Kanha reserve forest are of such type. They rarely put a halt in the normal wandering attitude of wild animals. In Gir forest some native Indians even communicate with big cats by producing special types of sound. The fellow lion understands such dialogue and gives a way out. It is a best example of the coexistence of people and animal with an aspiration of sharing the commonly available resources.

Most common thing about tiger is their affinity of remaning in places which remain beyond the reach of human beings. If we say that we are helping a tiger in leading a normal life by offering them a living in a confined area , then such claim may not satisfy the actual meaning of animal rights in a broader spectrum.

Native Indians are more adjusted to the forest than compared to the adjustment of their mind and emotions with the modern world. They prefer remaining isolated from the stream of industrialised development because of their adherence and trust upon the forest biota. They also consider themselves as an inseparable part of the greenery. This relationship of native Indians and forest can be ascribed more prominently by pointing out some incidents from any of the locations from some outskirts of Indian forest reserves.

Khokro village is located at the foothills of Dalma range of forest. The nearby industrial settlement of Tatanagar makes it more prominent and more prosperous. But the Paharia community residing in this village remained off the track of mainstreaming because of their lack of adequate faith in the development initiatives led by the government. People residing there prefer in keeping themselves contented through interacting with the surrounding and earning a living from the bundles usually they harvest. Most frequent invader of the village are wild elephants, beasts and some snakes. Bhanu, a Paharia child, learned to move these wilder animals out of village in various play way methods. He had even developed several mechanism of driving elephants out of the crop field without putting the animal much in trouble.

Government, under the leadership of a young development officer, took a stand to renovate the homes of tribal community by offering them cemented house. The traditional mud huts of all residents of the village were replaced by cemented heap of concrete. The fellow contractor made it quite differently. Most of the parts of houses remained unfinished. Poor performance of the contractor resulted in the seepage of rain water through cemented roofs.

The village elder, grandpa of Bhanu, has decided to visit the young officer to manage some support to make works finished. The strange report came out of the cabinet of the fellow officer. On the basis of that paper the assigned works of construction of all the sixty houses of Khokro village were considered as works completed successfully. This news made the inmates of village a bit confused. They had no voice to bring out their claims of surpassing miserable rainy days.

Chotulal, the only educated member of the community, approached a teacher of the nearby Ashram school and discussed about the problem in detail with him. Masterji moved on to meet the officer to enquire about the issue.

"I have a completion report," the standpoint of the officer made Masterji little bit unhappy. He was more unhappy by listening a claim of the officer regarding his rights.

"You have no right to go through minutes of the scheme. They must come and see. " The officer made his standpoint absolutely clear.

It compelled Masterji to move on for respecting the faith of Paharia people on him regarding his stand point of arbitration. The officer and his men wanted to bring back Masterji on the discussion table, but his superimposed egoistic motive force compelled him in not doing the same. It was more configurative in covering up the instances of some corrupt practices having deep involution of impulse from top to bottom.

The file of Paharias prepared by Masterji passed on a strict concern up to the table of higher officials.

"Namaste! Can I speak to Masterji?", The strange voice vibrated the eardrum of a performer of Meditation and Yoga.

"I'm the person you are talking about. Please come." Masterji welcomed the stranger gladly.

"I am from the Division office…"

"What can I do for you, Sir?"

"Very simple, you have to withdraw the case and tell your men to diffuse the tension."

"Tension!"

"Actually we all know, those innocent tribal people cannot draft any arbitrary documentation without involvement of any Master mind."

"You are at wrong place. Your officer told me that ....."", Masterji continued explaining the way development officer behaved during his visit. He was not even ready to listen to him and his men from Khokro village.

The news of the visit of Divisional officer and the case of unfinished housings spread in and around the area. Political leaders also came in action. Shankari Prasad, another tribal leader of that locality had some prominent hold on the local people, instructed Chotulal to cooperate with Masterji by all means. Because of that reason other prominent leaders having direct or indirect relations in the local area remained off the track. Paharia people even refused to talk to ministers. They had only a confirmed standpoint of remaining aside Masterji.

"We have arranged a meeting, sir..", the voice of the divisional officer was pitched down, "We request you to attend the same.. Our vehicles and our men will be there to lift you, sir."

The kindness of those officers is because of the fact that villagers refused to talk to them in absence of Masterji. Day by day the situation started transforming into more critical one. Divisional officer stayed there for two days to reach any remedial efforts which may lead them towards resolving the tension. Ultimately agreement made in terms of the mutual stand point of finishing the work followed by withdrawal of the petition.

"This is my second approach to you , Sir.", development officer appeared again after a gap of four months. It was the period after the completion of all construction works as per the proposed parameters and standards. Some additional units were added in it. Whitewashing of the entire unite was also made by officers and their corps to make their higher authority convinced.

Masterji moved on to think about withdrawing the petition after consulting Chotulal, Shankari Prasad and fellow Paharia people of Khokro. It was a day of victory for villagers. Credit and praise was there for Masterji. He was the only master mind to make people think about delivering their duties with proper affinity of making welfare of innocent villagers possible. It was also an act of winning, retaining and cultivating the faith of people on the system of governance.

In the modern society, everything happens as per the definite format of action and communication that people of certain area and certain community designed for them. They even worship their divine master on the format that previously designed for them with an aspiration of implementing a collective progress.

Here lies the principle of an integrated development of the community and development of a nation as a whole. The country having a balanced format of linking people with a system through sanctions and propositions then chances of sustained progress will become accelerated by multiple fold. It will even keep people at the good faith of the government.

People should have adequate affinity of remaining linked with others. Oppressions of any type and any level should not be tolerated at this leel at the cost of the loss of people's confidence upon the system. Any country spending on defense with an aspiration of keeping people at good faith. All the nations spending on their defense may rarely indulge in any organised battle at any war front. Then also they go on purchasing advanced weapons only for enhancing confidence of people on a system. Countries having a democratic status are generally exhibit their collective ambitions through planned ations of all types. Here also leaders and officials work to link people together through feeling that their ambitions, wishes and aspirations are duly materialised.

Properly linked people can put their wishes, ambitions and aspirations together to help their government in overcoming the problems of any type. People of Armenia living in other countries exhibited their will power by declaring their participation in the war imposed upon their nation by some other adjoining states. With such collective aspirations they started moving in for redefining their respective roles in the armed forces of their nation. It was an example of the exhibit of nationalism of highest order.

In modern times different electronic media prevalent in the society are working as an open platform for linking people on the basis of any issues and concerns. Because of that networked apprehension of the community the waves of the community feelings on certain issues start becoming visible immediately. People remaining linked to such electronic media often face difficulties in conferring their views appropriately because of their inability of expressing properly in the electronically empowered platform. Some other oppressive factors are working in this field by keeping them off the screen. Then also electronic media is becoming a balanced exhibit of the waves of community feelings.

Agencies of investigations, law enforcements and politics started depending upon the electronic media and social media to a greater extent for working out their own strategies and plan of actions. These instruments also make them competent enough in implementing certain santions and law enforcement resolutions at a large scale. People of India agetated with high degree of anger when the news from Line of Actual Control duly came where the great warrior of Indian Army Santosh Babu and few other friends lost their lives during one of the brute attack implemented by armed forces of China during the month of June. People demanded a counter attack and also started demanding a quick and rapid action. Entire world became stunned of the act of China. Diffusion of the tension went on through bilateral talks and side by side both the country started preparing themselves for some highest order of combat.

As evident from the Gita, warrior Arjun lost his balance of mind after seeing his master, his elders and other relatives standing on the opponent's side. He refused to kill his masters and relatives simply for gaining a state. He even expressed his desire to cast off all his wishes to stop such a mass killing.

Such a state of confusion comes during a loss of proper coordination between the mind and intellect. One may lose any challenge immediately if they impart themselves in any action by keeping such a state of confusion in mind. The stand of Arjuna amidst the battle field was vividly explained by lord Krishna. There developed the conversation of Krishna with Arjuna to enlighten the role of Pandavas in the battle. As parent, grand parents, friends and masters joining the opponent sides had not delivered their duties properly they all lost their special status and became a culprit responsible for the development of tension and conflicts, which ultimately led two different segments of the same family to declare war against each other.

Such a state of confusion developed in the mind of Arjun because of his state of attachement with fellow relatives, masters, friends, brothers and sisters who were joining the opponent side and were planning to hold and use weapons against Pandavas, the five brothers including Arjun.

At this critical juncture lord Krishna explained the essence of maintaining balance of mind by bringing out oneself from the state of confusion through gaining true knowledge. There exists a clear distinction between the soul of the individual and the respective physical body. Physical body may perish, elements present in bodily organs may disintegrate, physicaaly the body may die, but waves and propositions of the soul will remain active in this world for centuries. In forthcoming days people may remember them through their acts, attitudes and conducts.

After knowing such differences and knowing about the importance of perfectly planned actions in life Arjun gradually prepared himself for the war. Entire Gita is the exhibit of the journey of Arjun from the state of confusion, sorrow and agony to the state of self confidence, self esteem and enlightenment. At his ultimate state of awareness he felt the presence of the Divine beside himself; it was also there within himself. His failure in feeling such an omnipresence was due to lack of true knowledge only. It was also due to his unwanted attachment to the physical world and worldly things.

Open Discussion

We are at the final stage of our discussion on Yoga. Here comes a moment when we try to consider some of the live experiences from different walks of life. Some of the events were reported by various historians and thinkers time to time. We cannot claim the exactness of all such events. It is obviously claimed that all of these events bear some clear message regarding waves of the thought process with which human beings lead a fruitful life.

A Burning Candle

Being a good student Sarkaar was popular amongst his fellow classmates. After few of the contact classes even Dr. Spandan came to know about in. For availing few more clarifications on selected topics Sarkar received a call to visit professor's house along with some of his fellow friends.

Student teacher relation of such type during eighties was really a matter of great concern, when most of fellow teachers started infusing their desires for having easy access to bundles of currency.

"Sarkar, if you feel any trouble in grasping the concept, just come and tell me. A prosperous doctor should have an eagerness to know the inter-relations of organs and system.

It is obviously vital for you. ", The instruction of a teacher was absolutely clear.

Sarkar and his other three friends remained silent for admitting their agreement in attending some special session at the residence of Prof. Spandan.

There started a series of discussion, analysis and experimentation. Another fellow member of the family greeted the spark of Sarkar differently for assigning some smaller duties to confirm the sure visit of Sarkar on a daily basis. It was Kalyani, the beloved daughter of the professor.

"Would you like to bring a packet of bakery snacks for me?", Kalyani approached Sarkar from the inwardly aligned doorsteps of the inner quarter.

There was a prompt reply, "Sure."

Only the person who remained in dark for not having an opportunity to witness the apprehension of Kalyani for seeing and admiring the presence of a fellow student of absolute genre in her courtyard on a daily basis.

Days and months passed on in the way it had to. A couple of souls got an opportunity to admit the need of another one for the self. Sarkar started meeting Kalyani with a bit differences. During his prolonged absence from the college because of the illness of his grandpa, Kalyani started feeing a kind of twist and spins in her mind and body that started offering her some discomfort.

Professor marked the progress in a different apprehensive proposition and decided to issue a strict warning for

Sarkaar. The very next morning after the prolonged absence of Sarkaar from doubt clearing session some permanent doubts remained buried in his mind after receiving some clear instructions from his fellow professor, "Actually you know Sarkaar! I am not feeling myself much comfortable to tell you something about my Kalyani. She spends a lot. We are also allowing her to do so. The person who intends to attend her should have such capabilities to spend through. Being a fellow from a middle class one should prefer keeping a distance from a fire. "

Sarkaar preferred keeping his silence and also decided not to disclose the critical state of his mind regarding his regular visit to professor's house.

"Even her beauty equipment comes from some foreign companies ..", Professor continued narrating some of the aspects of the standard of the life his daughter was making herself habituated for.

There developed a need of altering the venue of arranging doubt clearing session. Special impression about the fellow student duly diffused for few months. Declaration of the final result of graduation made the fellow professor a bit unhappy. There mounted a sorrow even on the face of Kalyani. This time Bhubaneswari, the mother of that fellow girl was more active. The incident was regarding the fact that Sarkaar stood first in the graduation examination. Not only that, he became a gold medalist. It had also confirmed his service life. The government may approach Sarkaar to join the same Medical College as a professor.

Coming under pressure from most of the family members, Professor Spandan took his vehicle and instructed his driver to trace out the native place of Sarkar. Without making delay he wanted to meet him in person. By that time the middle class fellow approached an agency for scholarship and started preparations to move abroad for some higher studies. His intention struck to the point of attaining the supreme position in the medical profession in terms of knowledge enrichment and compassion of delivering quality services. The kind of standpoint of Sarkaar made the possibilities of bringing back the happiness of Kalyani feeble. The last chance was even blotted out during his last time conversation with the beloved professor, "actually sir, I have decided to move abroad for higher studies. I also expect your blessings."

The kind voice of his fellow student has melted the egoistic motive of Professor Spandan. His voice went on slipping down while passing some of the instructions and timely important tips regarding collection of some references which may become helpful for the fellow student while staying abroad. Notion regarding Kalyani remained off the scene because the strict standpoint of Sarkaar. His firmness and deeper adherence to the profession and knowledge made professor confident enough in guessing about his exit from the Indian context. Because of this reason he remained off the scene to admit the situation of Kalyani.

There remained silence in the courtyard for few years for having no scope of replacing Sarkaar by any other fellow. A gap of unbearable four years passed on. Marriage ceremony for Kalyani duly arranged for making an effort to make her happy. The appointed fellow was competent enough in fulfilling the thirst of wealth and prosperity of the fellow girl. The happiness that snatched by the gentle smile and kind looking of Sarkaar remained off the track. Kalyani rarely received any confession room for admitting her situation of unrest and unhappy. Such kind of discontentment made her sicker, more rigid and less cooperative.

Sarkaar got an opportunity to sharpen his intellect. There also he had managed to secure his position of a sincere fellow. It was a smooth completion of his advanced studies of surgery and allied science. There also he started receiving offers from various colleges and universities to join as a faculty. It was a scope of gain for the fellow doctor in terms of money and fame, on the other hand it was a strand of sliding from his commitment to serve the motherland. Sarkar decided to return to his native place. He had also decided to impart himself in nation building efforts by all means.

The stand of Sarkaar made his professor more uncomfortable. Professor wanted to meet Sarkaar in person. Ultimately the gatekeeper and Bhaja, the only servant allowed professor to sit and wait for his turn. There were more than a hundred patient. Bhaja was little bit unaware of the faceted relationships of professor and his fellow student. It was also an opportunity for professor to wait and watch the activities of his beloved student. One can rarely keep faith upon the way Sarkaar took a stand of serving his motherland by remaining absolutely unconditional. It had perpetuated all thinking of professor regarding the attitude of Sarkaar towards the motherland and towards the countrymen. He came back only for serving people.

Ultimately the turn came, "Let me see you properly my boy, first!." Professor took Sarkaar near his shoulder and his glistening eyes started exploring some safest place to drop tears which started rolling down from the lines of vision. It was absolutely his fault which has taken away Kalyani from the life of Sarkaar.

"I've lost my gem, you know!"

"What happened to you , sir?"

"Actually I thought you will never return. As nobody turns back. There developed new arrangements for Kalyani."

"Nothing wrong in it, Sir. "

"Everything was wrong, why not!"

"You see! My status, my power, my patients. I have nothing special to give her."

"She is not happy there", professor continued talking to make Sarkaar attentive about the situation of Kalyani. At least he should express his desire to see her. The coin tossed differently and the affinity of Sarkaar towards his job, his pupil made professor confident enough regarding the lifestyle of Sarkaar. He came back with a heavy mind inflicted utterly with sorrow. It was even more and more unbearable situation as It had fainted the possibility of making Kalyani happy.

During one fine morning the news of the last breathe of Kalyani came. It has developed a silence in the courtyard of the residence for Sarkaar. Professor witnessed the mounting of sorrow on the face of Sarkaar. It was bit unbearable for him. He started considering himself responsible for the kind of loss. His rigidity and firmness of not to settle issues with Professor made him less accountable. He had arranged a heavy and powerful planners for planning and submitting schemes potent enough in delivering duties. Kalyani managed to escape the turmoil of reverse current of life which has tossed for her differently because of lack of Sarkaar.

Absence of Kalyani intensified the wish of the fellow doctors to do something fruitful for bringing her alive and making her breathe.

"Think about yourself, Sarkaar. Go for a prosperous life. That will be a real tribute to your beloved ones." Professor started convincing Sarkaar for indulging in a fruitful family life. It had no impression in the mind of the fellow young patriot who developed a passion of making his motherland prosperous, generous and resourceful.

"First of all I want to make Kalyani alive, sir. Let us join hands to make it a reality." The standpoint of Sarkaar became clear to his fellow teacher. Sarkaar prepared himself for mission accomplishment through political indulgence. He gained adequate public support due to his brilliant service record. His position in the State Assembly secured the position of supreme leader for him. It was the turning point from which he has decided to move forward to make Kalyani alive at plenty of instances. City, bridge, hospital, welfare schemes and some other new developments, all such efforts were dedicated to Kalyani. All such development went on in the name of Kalyani. These efforts made Kalyani alive for Sarkaar. Professor was not so competent in feeling such efforts as any measure of gaining pleasure. The wet corners of his eye intended to convince Sarkaar for a prosperous family life.

Sarkaar engaged himself in nation building efforts to keep Kalyani breathe for the millions. Nobody questioned him for putting the name Kalyani besides any new venture. His wish greeted by fellow associates gladly to apprehend his happiness. These efforts turned into worship for Sarkaar. All such efforts duly witnessed by his fellow teacher made him more contented because of his ability to keep Kalyani active even deep inside his mind and intellect. In due course of time Kalyani became his life blood, an accomplishable effort, a kind of desirable pleasure, a moment of utter peace and contentment. Such a feeling enjoyed by Sarkaar through his entire life propositions. He has decided to keep such efforts alive in due course of time.

Belogingness to Nature

Khokro village is located at the foothills of Dalma range of forest. The nearby industrial settlement of Tatanagar makes it more prominent and more prosperous. But the Paharia community residing in this village remained off the track of mainstreaming because of their lack of adequate faith in the development initiatives led by the government. People residing there prefer in keeping themselves contented through interacting with the surrounding and earning a living from the bundles usually they harvest. Most frequent invader of the village are wild elephants, beasts and some snakes. Bhanu, a Paharia child, learned to move these wilder animals out of village in various play way methods. He had even developed several mechanism of driving elephants out of the crop field without putting the animal in harm.

Government under the leadership of a young development officer took a stand to renovate the homes of tribal community by offering them cemented house. The traditional mud huts of all residents of the village were replaced by cemented heap of concrete. The fellow contractor made it quite differently. Most of the parts of houses remained unfinished. Poor performance of the contractor resulted in the seepage of rain water through cemented roofs.

The village elder, grandpa of Bhanu, has decided to visit the young officer to manage some support to make works finished. The strange report came out of the cabinet of the fellow officer. The assigned works of construction of all the sixty houses of Khokro village were completed successfully. This news made the inmates of village a bit confused. They had no voice to bring out their claims of surpassing miserable rainy days.

Chotulal, the only educated member of the community approached a teacher of the nearby Ashram school and discussed about the problem in detail with him. Masterji moved on to meet the officer to enquire about the issue.

"I have a completion report," the standpoint of the officer made Masterji little bit unhappy. He was more unhappy by listening a claim of the officer regarding his rights.

"You have no right to go through minutes of the scheme. They must come and see. " The officer made his standpoint absolutely clear.

It compelled Masterji to move on for respecting the faith of Paharia people on him regarding his stand point of arbitration. The officer and his men wanted to bring back Masterji on the discussion table, but his superimposed egoistic motive force compelled him in not doing the same. It was more configurative in covering up the instances of some corrupt practices having deep involution of impulse from top to bottom.

The file of Paharias prepared by Masterji passed on a strict impulse up to the table of higher officials.

"Namaste! Can I speak to Masterji?", The strange voice vibrated the eardrum of a performer of Meditation and Yoga.

"I'm the person you are talking about. Please come." Masterji welcomed the stranger gladly.

"I am from the Division office…"

"What can I do for you, Sir?"

"Very simple, you have t owithdraw the case and tell your men to diffuse the tension."

"Tension!"

"Actually we all know, those innocent tribal people cannot draft any arbitrary documentation without involvement of any Master mind."

"You are at wrong place. Your officer told me that .....",
Masterji continued explaining the way development officer
behaved during his visit. He was not even ready to listen to
him and his men from Khokro village.

The news of the visit of Divisional officer and the case of
unfinished housings spread in and around the area.
Political leaders also came in action. Shankari Prasad,
another tribal leader of that locality had some prominent
hold on the local people, instructed Chotulal to cooperate
with Masterji by all means. Because of that reason other
prominent leaders having direct or indirect relations in the
local area remained off the track. Paharia people even
refused to talk to ministers. They had only a confirmed
standpoint of remaining aside Masterji.

"We have arranged a meeting, sir..", the voice of the
divisional officer was pitched down, "We request you to
attend the same.. Our vehicles and our men will be there to
lift you, sir."

The kindness of those officers is because of the fact that
villagers refused to talk to them in absence of Masterji.
Day by day the situation started transforming more critical.
Divisional officer stayed there for two days to reach any
remedial efforts of resolving the tension. Ultimately
agreement made in terms of the mutual stand point of
finishing the work followed by withdrawal of the petition.

"This is my second approach to you , Sir.", development
officer appeared again after a gap of four months. It was
the period after the completion of all construction works
as per the proposed parameters and standards. Some
additional units were added in it. Whitewashing of the

entire unite was also made by officers and their corps to make their higher authority convinced.

Masterji moved on to think about withdrawing the petition after consulting Chotulal, Shankari Prasad and fellow Paharia people of Khokro. It was a day of victory for villagers. Credit and praise was there for Masterji. He was the only master mind to make people think about delivering their duties with proper affinity of making welfare of innocent villagers possible. It was also an act of winning, retaining and cultivating the faith of people on the system of governance.

Strong Determination

"I am Bani. You can reach me any time through your handset. So without delay just do it…", these familiar dialects can make any of the prosperous boy little bit restless. They prefer entering the caht room immediately. Pre recoded voice can even make them contented.

There was a person from the other side who wanted to reach Baani in person to have some live experiences. He had a developed a deep feeling for the girl. He started approaching the fellow girl through the chat room. Baani was obviously a good looking one. She had a glamorous look, a firmness on her physique, a moderate curving with big naturals. Her voice was also quite sweet.

She got the appointment in the chatroom because of her beautiful eyes and soft voice. She had to attend visitors of the chat room as per the recommendations of the manager of the chat room. She was even free to attend the chatting as per her own convenience. There was a system of arranging time for people having affinity to go for a prolonged discussion with Baani.

The fellow boy namely Durjan was from a semi urban settlement located near Gwalior. He had a prosperous business empire. After appointing a manager to look after daily transactions, he had managed enough time to indulge in non –productive activities like chatting, dating etc. indulging in chatting with Baani made him restless. He was feeling such kind of strange development in himself. Without meeting Baani in person the problem of such feelings may continuously put on disturbing him.

After collecting all particulars about the chatting center and their office details Durjan decided to move on towards the city office located at Noida. After a long discussion the manager of the chat room provided her the address and contact number of Baani.

"Baani! Hello… ", the voice of Durjan was recognized by the fellow girl.

"Yes, I'm."

"Actually you know! I want to meet you. I have some talks that I may not be able to discuss in open. So would you like to have such time for me?"

"At this moment, I have no free time. Later on I can think upon."

"OK, then you can save my contact number. By the way, I'm a business man from nearby township of Gwalior, my .. ", he was stopped in the middle by the fellow girl.

Baani was not in a position to discuss all the particulars about her regarding the types of complications that drifts her every moments from avoiding the chance of meeting any members of the chatting room in person.

Ultimately the day came. It was near Noida itself. Baani provided free moment for Durjan. The third seat alongside the table was occupied by the fellow manager. It was little bit annoying for Durjan. After all first time any girl may not agree upon meeting any stranger alone at any public place. Because of that reason also presence of manager at the discussion table was granted by Durjan. What made him more annoying was the way manager started serving coffees and snacks to all the three places.

With certain business tricks Durjan floated an offer for the fellow girl, "actually I want to make you my Brand Symbol for my various hotels located at some of the big cities. If you agree upon then we can discuss about the package and other benefits."

"For that what you want me to do?"

"Simple! You have to opt for some of my add clips. My media persons visit you for taking such clips. And if possible you have to visit those of my hotels, madam."

"No Madam, Baani."

"OK, Baani!"

Durjan floated his plan of developing further closeness with the fellow girl of substance.

She had decided to opt for the package alongside the involvement of the manager of the chatting room. She wanted to ensure the presence of her friend alongside the other.

Situation turned around differently after entry of her another assistant governess, who used to look after her daily activities. She was there to provide her newly mended sandals. One of the sandal was little bit swollen and had bigger attachments than compared to that of the normal one. The kind of sudden entry of the governess implanted a silence in the room. The speechless mood of Durjan was drifted off by the soft notion of the manager, "one of the leg of Baani is artificial one. Due to that reson…"

"So what! These days people do many things with both the limbs amputated", Durjan also buried all his desires to exhibit some of his beautiful proposals. A sorrow mixed with fainted happiness mounted upon the face of Durjan.

The meeting concluded with a confirmation of Baani and that of the fellow manager to come across promoting the hospitality services of Durjan.

Durjan decided to burry his desires within his heart and moved on after confirming the agreement of Baani on his business proposals. The relationship of Bani and Durjan restricted up to the business deals only. Chances of any further development of the relation remained fainted. Baani got the point and shifted herself off the chances of having any further meeting related to her involvement in the process of her indulgence in the branding process. She had placed the fellow manager forward for bypassing the chances of further meetings with Durjan.

It was her habitual motive force. She had adjusted herself in exhibiting the parts only meant for drawing attention of others towards her. She had even ignored the chances of any exhibits of the specially enabled body parts in near future. Her aspirations of continuing her service in near future compelled her to share some of her emotions to attend those of other visitors of the chatting room. It remained her band of organized actions for a considerable period of time. She was not even in a position to earn any sympathy from any other friendly persons. She had enough capabilities of exploring the chances of drifting her desires towards proving her abilities and skills.

A River Without Confluence

The news of the birth of a girl child made most of the family members quite unhappy. They were expecting birth of a male child. Most joyous expression of the father of that baby made all people witnessing the process quite confused. The fact is that the face of the girl child is exactly a carbon copy of her father. Father Mohanlal was also in a fix to offer adequate care to make his girl more prosperous in her later life. She should have adequate access to scope of learning, dancing, drawing and painting. Whatever field liked by the fellow girl child her father used to provide her.

Mohan had even shifted his family to nearby city for avoiding unwanted attendance of nearby people and inmates in the form of some bad touches, molestations etc. making inmates stop from doing such thigs is quite difficult. Implying a strong vigil and not allowing her to have some play way indulgence with cousins may make others unhappy, so better was to shift her to a safest quarter.

Specially appointed teachers, special guards, exclusive vehicles and many more facilities deployed at the place for enabling her swift and soft continuation of study. Her results started reflecting the caring nature of her beloved father. The entire consent of the fellow girl got the presence of the caring nature of her father. She had rarely any free time to think upon other issues beyond the scope of studies.

"Sheela! Where are you?" Mohan started calling Sheela just after entering the main door of the quarter.

"My God, so many books!" The stack of different books carried by her father made the prosperous girl excited. All the books filled up her entire table. It has also drifted her interest towards the subject matter. Stories, maps, wonders, Universe, Science, Maths and so many different topics made Sheela entirely contented. Mohan was a bit particular in selecting topics to be handed over to the fellow girl. Her brain mapping started taking shape in accord to the isuues and concerns floated for her by her sharing and caring parents.

Mother of the prosperous girl child was even more attentive in addressing all the need of the fellow girl. They parents had lot of passion for offering a friendly environment for their ward to enable her to relocate herself amidst the turmoil of varying degrees and extent.

Days started passing on and Sheela also moved on through her teenage to come across her days of success to reach up to the university life. Medical university located at Delhi was her new destiny. She made herself deeply involved in the study of surgical particulars of her interest. If any individual wants to make oneself attentive and contented then success will be at the doorstep, Sheela is one such example.

Amidst all the prosperity and success, one thing, which was lacking in the progressive trend of the life of fellow girl, made her parents worried considerably. She had never even developed any intimate relationship with any of her boyfriends. She often attends party, meets friends, enters chat rooms, floats her profile on net, but at all instances she start speaking on oncogenes, carcinogens and all such topics of her interest and of the field of medical science.

One fellow namely Mark, an Anglo fellow, agreed upon proposal of parents of Sheela to talk about establishing a marital relation with the fellow girls. That time Sheela was preparing her synopsis of a forthcoming research project. She had to submit the same in time. The date o f seminar was culminated with that of the date given by Mark. It was duly rejected by the fellow girl at her thirty. Another four years drifted the situation towards a turmoil of the death of her grandpa. She had no option for talking about her engagement rings.

Another Marathi fellow, a professor in the same research institute, proposed his name during one of the party meet to have an interest in establishing a bond of permanent friendship with the fellow girl. It made her parents more contented and they were in their motive of discussing the same issue during their free time at the dinner table. That time the familiar ring of the Marathi fellow namely Dhananjay came. Her father took the call and invited him to have a dinner party along with them. Sheela remained ignorant of such initiatives of her parents.

What was not of the expectation ,only that thing continued on the dinner table while Dhananjay and Sheela engaged in discussion. For most of the time they remained in their topic filled with medical terms, departmental problems and some other research related topics. Dhananjay agreed upon helping her to continue her research activities. It went on through such hardships of exchange of views. The main topic of establishing, maintaining and conferring the development of marital relations kept aside.

Sheela buried her sexual urge of all kinds for making her life contented one through attaining success in her research activities.

Dhanajay and Sheela started dating each other. All sorts of dating remained restricted in the efforts of finding out the ways and means of making the research activities of the fellow girl a successful one. For the purpose of the forthcoming advance studies and also for impairing herself for delivering guest lectures in foreign universities she started moving abroad frequently. This time also, most cooperative, most responsible and most service providing person was her father.

Her personal life remained filled with ambitions, responsibilities and explorations inflicted with the subject matter upon which she was concentrating most frequently.

Her utter indulgence in the field of studies made her quite unfit in establishing any deeper friendship with any of her boyfriends. Dhanajay was a little bit different than other members of the institute.

Family members of the Marathi fellow came to know about the move of Sheela to some foreign universities of some high profile. They have decided to opt for some other bond for their Dhanajay. It came in the notice of Sheela's father after a couple of month. After knowing such stand of the family members of Dhanajay, Mohan was not happy. He again started searching some better alternative for his girl in different sources linked with add agencies, dailies and some other friend circles.

There came a strict warning from his daughter, "You please stop searching anything further, dad. I've decided not to opt for any one."

Her father agreed upon the stand of Sheela. It was quite difficult to stop the urge of her mother. For stopping her mother from exploring anything absurd for her she had decided to put a difficult condition for her to be life partners. The condition was very simple, "anybody willing to establish a marital bond with me, he should pay half the cost of my flat also agree upon staying with us at our home. I cannot go to other's house. The person should come to that of mine.

Moreover, he should not put me off my service. "

It made her mom little bit relieved. After all her daughter agreed upon finding out a person having such passion of moving through searching out any alternative of gaining the confidence of Sheela.

Mohan took the side of her prosperous girl. He has decided to move on for providing all possible support to his girl of substance. Sheela should receive some moral, some emotional and some timely support. She started receiving a big amount from different job profiles. Her publications also moved on for gaining a big audience. Her profile registered millions of views. All these progress kept only one thing away, chances of any male member from her known circle to have a permanent marital bond with the fellow girl of high profile. Her contentment upon the services and her multinational character drifted her father off the regular service. Mohan became a regular partner of the experimental pathological lab meant for conducting experimental research activities.

A girl having such stand of keeping aside all sexual urge for fulfilling some higher purpose in life made Sheela a unique amongst all. She continued in exploring her possibilities by keeping her eyes on the microscopes and relying entirely upon the timely support of her father for experimenting upon something challenging.

The way Sheela spent her life never put her in trouble due to infiltration of any sexual urge of any type. Some of the past experiences made her confirmed about her capabilities of attaining success within a stipulated timeframe.

A saint from South India had a beautiful dream. Lord Shiva wanted to establish himself in a temple constructed and maintained by the saint. His financial condition was not much better, that is why planning and spending any big amount to construct a temple was beyond his reach. In another way person can construct a temple. Ultimately god also resides in the mind of his follower. This reality paved a path for the poor saint. He started making his dream more and more profound and more and more concrete. He has also received support of the fellow villagers of adjoining areas. Due to the firmness of the saint more and more people started keeping faith on him. His plan of making the temple in dream remained continuing amidst the continuity of the worships duly conducted by villagers. Fellow villagers accompanied the saint in his continuing worship underneath a banyan tree.

The entire thing became public in a short period of time. King of the same territory was also a devotee of Lord Shiva. He had also a beautiful dream of constructing a temple and offering it to his lord. He had got a holy message of his lord in the form of another dream. Lord ordered him to arrange the needful for ensuring construction of a temple in his kingdom.

King's generals informed him about the uninterrupted worship of Lord Shiva which was going on under the able guidance of the saint. They are offering food to the hungry ones, clothes to poor ones and water to thirsty ones. Serving living things is considered by them eqal to serving god. They are also offering water to newly placed saplings. If these activities remain continuing, then, it is obvious that, they will gain prosperity in a short period of time.

Learning the fact in a rapid progression king wanted to move on to meet the saint. The kind of information duly conveyed to the fellow villagers. Same information in the form of a royal command came to the saint too, instructing him not to leave the place without informing generals deputed there at the service of the empire.

The way information of the arrival of the king came to them were little bit scary. Everybody started guessing various possible fates of the admission of their king in a poor village. Fellow villagers had even nothing in special to welcome their judiciary lord. They remained at the service of their divine lord.

Saintly person inflicted entirely with a divine dream decided not to pay adequate attention to the messenger, who warned him not to leave the place. The kind of warning was issued on the basis of the order issued by the royal court in the name of generals. Villagers were also in a fix to go on worshipping the way they wanted to do. Nothing special change in the series of activities became observable due to firmness of the fellow devotees of Lord Shiva. They were jointly decided to welcome their judiciary lord amidst the holy place of the banyan tree. They were also trying to gain confidence on themselves through offering all their wishes and worries to their beloved Divine Lord. This stand made them more confident about the ways and means they were adopting for worships.

Finally the day of the final meeting of two devotees of the Divine Lord came. They started discussion about their specific dream.

"You have decided to welcome Lord Shiva in your own temple?" King asked to the saint.

"The Temple is there in my dream only, My Lord." Soft voice of the saint drifted silence in the entire place beneath the banyan tree. Only some feeble chanting of hymns were radiating out in different directions from a distant place, where some people remained engaged in performing holy offerings.

"Let me know your dream, at least", king expressed his desire of becoming acquainted of the specific dream of the saint.

Discussion went on for a long time. Ultimately they came to know about the similarity of their dreams. They went on constructing the temple in dream, as well as in reality.

Problem developed due to the stand of saint. He wanted to welcome the Divine God in his own temple. He was not in a position to accommodate his beloved master of mind in the temple of some other fellow.

"I am ready to donate the temple to you. It is only your dream came true, my master. Please accept the same. If you wish, something more can be added to the construct." The kind appeal of king made the entire process a confluent one. There was no debate regarding any claim upon the ownership of the holy temple. In terms of the wealth it was owned by the king. In terms of devotion and divine pursuit, it was the temple of the saintly person. Finally the idol of Divine God was established in the temple with great enthusiasm. All the inmates of the royal family, and also inmates of the saintly family, took part in the ceremonial welcoming of the Divine God.

A War and Worship

Malla Dynasty of India is famous for its affinity towards implying prime importance upon the prosperity of people. For that reason the fellow kings of this dynasty maintained their adherence towards worship of the Divine. They had less affinity towards the expansion of the territory through war or any other war like conflicts. Then also they were maintaining a big army which was efficient enough in planning and winning any battle. Gopal Singh (the Warrior King) took the lead in popularising worship of Madan Mohan in his kingdom.

Once a Warrior King became famous amongst his men because of his devotion to the Master of all Masters. He had also constructed several beautiful temples in different parts of his kingdom for sheltering his masters. Temples of such types became very famous in localities. People started using such temples as their land mark signs. Not only that, some of the temples got the prominence as a market hub. Saintly persons started using these public places as their seats of religious purposes.

"Have you seen God?", one of the saint asked a youth.

Youth answered instantly, "Yes."

The kind of answer was somehow not expected.

"Where?", finally saint broke his silence.

"God is there in me. It is also there in you. The God is even speaking through you. Any customer is a God for shopkeepers. I am sure you are not getting confused.",

Smiling face of that youth stunned all the people watching the conversation.

Different other instances of this type became a normal affair of the temple corridors. Things were moving softly and peacefully. All things were not in peace. All places of the kingdom ware not equally protected. Some of the places of border areas often experienced invasion of different types by different groups of bad tempered people. Most of the time the invasion of grabbers made the king worried about his ward.

He has decided to become merciless to smash all the grabbers.

Grabbers never cultivate crops. They even never take part in making instruments. They are also less interested in joining other farmers for any support. They can do only one thing. Invade a village. Put people in trouble and harvest ripe crops.

The only loser because of such grabbers were farmers. The Warrior King has decided to organise a specially trained people of strong physique to tackle such grabbers and smash them instantly on the spot. The kind of firm action made all the grabbers worried. They were invading different territories of the kingdom in small groups. After the kind of firm action from the side of the kingdom all the grabbers decided to opt for joint actions. One such joint action made them victorious in a village located at the foothill of border areas.

The victory was only because of delays in reaching the information to the state capita.

"We construct high altitude towers at selected places in such a way that signals of lights and flags broadcasted from one tower should be visible from other towers. In this way we can get the information instantly with a speed of light.", The kind of instruction made all the engineers of the kingdom busy in implementing the dream plan within a short span of just one year.

Farmers may remain tension free by the end of the forthcoming crop season.

Name of such towers coined by gabbers is Temple Tower. They always remain scared of matters related to temple. The turn of grabbers came. They became more united, more violent, more particular and more refined.

Instruction of direct action was already issued to villagers of border areas of the kingdom. They have a special thing, namely Temple Tower, which can link them with the state capita instantly.

During one evening, soldiers deputed at the Temple Tower observed the advancement of a large group of armed men towards their territory. The volume of such advance was so big that one can rarely finish counting properly. It was near about five thousand grabbers advancing towards the state capital.

"We grab them all, smash them all!", oppressors advancing towards the state capital were shouting in a rhyming tune.

Already it was evening time. Information system of flag cannot work properly. Other towers rarely recognise the signals. Generals decided to replace flag signals with those of fire signals. The dark side of the Temple Tower got illuminated.

Luminous signal of one Temple Tower gave birth to such signals at the other. With an instantaneous speed the information of the invasion of grabbers reached the state capital.

The time was vital for the king. He was extremely busy in worshipping his King of All Kings. Even all generals were there to look after the arrangements. They all were scheduled themselves for offering services to saints. The order came in the form of illuminated signal of keeping silence about the progression of grabbers. All the soldiers deputed at Temple Towers were not expecting such a reply from the state capital. For confirming the message of keeping silence, the signal indicating the advancement of grabbers populated for the second time. The second time also the reply was the same.

Keeping silence, means inviting massacre. They people become violent just after invading the territory.

One should not keep the law in hand without the royal concern. It was the time for generals and other men to find a hide out for themselves. Advancement of grabbers towards the state capital made them more worried. The information was again passed on to the kingdom. Finally the team of oppressors reached the state capital by the end of the following evening.

A large camp of grabbers made the inmates of the royal court and the royal family worried about their survival. Getting feared of such intrusion, they approached the king.

"Say no to war. This time we are welcoming our God. With the same vigil we also welcome our enemy. Let us see what they want. If they want our then we also want the same." The king was fixed at his stand.

The pale faces of all the inmates became more fainted after listening their king. They were equally proud of their king because of his religious nature. The type of incident prompted all the inmates and generals of the kingdom to surrender all their worries at the disposal of the King of all Kings. The population in the royal temple courtyard increased considerably.

It was a moonlit night. It was also a special one in terms of activities and faiths.

The master mind of grabbers tossed differently to attend the royal court with their claim upon the entire kingdom. They were in a plan of throwing out the king for grabbing the entire kingdom at a single go. More alarming for them was the way they were treated on the way of their advancement. Fellow villagers and farmers offered them essentials willingly. It was more alarming that, none of the countrymen opposed the stand of their king. No war during worship of the King of all Kings was the only thing they wanted to follow to make their king more wiser.

Only a peaceful mind can worship properly. All the countrymen led their worship in the same tune. They also welcomed their enemy with adequate patience and calmness of their mind.

.

The grabber master ordered his men to wait for the span of the moonlit night. The next morning will be a sunset for the king and his fellow generals. They must quit silently. If they are not moving away, then the other fate will be fatal for them all. The grabber master was in a full confidence. He was enjoying the silver markings of the moonlit night. He was also roaming around to ascertain the security of his men of actions.

The echo of songs and chanting are audible from the farthest point of the forest. The grabber master was not understanding the stand of king. He had no information about the peaceful stand of his opponent. That is why it was not sensible for them. He was also not confident about the policy of the king for not getting indulge in any war during any holy festival.

Two riders approaching the main gate of the fort of kingdom caught the vision of the grabber master and his selected generals.

"The king conspires something special for us." The grabber master said. He has issued an alert for his secret agents duly deputed at the place. "We must imply a close look upon them."

A gap of a couple of hour was the moment of the high pitched chanting and singing which was radiating out in the form of waves from the fort. That night the fort turned into a sacred temple of the King of all Kings. The Warrior King was the center of attention. All the inmates and generals forgot about the advancement of the grabbers. They have diffused their worries. The only thing remained in front of them was the smiling face of the King of all Kings.

All on a sudden a large ball of fire smashed one of the camp of the grabbers. There was no chance of escape. The same thing happened repeatedly in the midst of the mild darkness.

"Can you see the men the king is having?" The grabber master expressed his anger. He had no preparation for putting an instant reply in action. It was so sudden and so rapid that the entire team lost their rhythm in a short span of an hour.

After coming out og the nearby hideouts, the grabber master wanted to assess the nature and extent of the damage. Only men less than five hundred were in a position to stand upon their own. They had no medications for curing wounded ones. It was also a state of utter confusion. More shameful was the act of only two men who smashed the entire team of grabbers.

Finally, the grabber king changed his mind and decided to meet the king.

The onset of morning made the dream of the grabbers a matter of high risk. How to escape the territory became a challenge for them. Surrendering at the feet of king was the only way out. The Warrior King remained involved in the worship of the King of all Kings.

The grabber master came at the door step of the fort to admit his mistakes. He also expressed his desire of putting his arms down.

"I am a great failure, my king. Only the thing I want is that men. I want to see them. I've never seen such brave warriors. Once I want to see them. Please accept our humble request."

The type of request made by the grabber master was something strange for the king. It also made the king unhappy. He started searching the person who has violated his appeal.

"All the generals, please find the culprits. They should furnish reasons."

Actually there was nothing to search. All the generals and men were standing in front of their king. Who will search whom? The Warrior King ascertained the fact and answered the grabber master politely, "Actually there are nothing to search. All men are here only. So nobody used fireballs from our side. You may please find them at some other place."

The only evidence alive was the horses kept at the main gate. There were traces of fireworks lying here and there at the hinder part of the courtyard. Somebody has used canons. The question arises about the way they might have entered the main campus of the fort for taking the hold of the powerful canons. After raining fireballs on the enemy they even more silently left the place.

"The horses, your highness…" , the grabber master admitted his eagerness to see those generals. The appeal remained unattended from the royal side.

Only the thing remained in the mind of grabbers was in the form of a faith upon some supreme force that saved the kingdom just before the advent of utter destruction.

Grabber master got the final lesson in the form of caring attendance of the Warrior King. He has received essential items duly required for the days they surpass inside the territory. Generals and other villagers must not put them in any trouble. It was the noble treatment to the enemy who wanted to grab the entire country.

Once again the wave of green flags indicated the advent of peace in the entire territory of the Warrior King.

The Salt Merchant

Chayan Vyapari was a famous Salt Merchant from India. He was famous, not only for his expanded business empires. He was not only famous for his ability of involving tirelessly in his day to day activities. His ability of remaining simple along with extraordinary characters made him more popular. He used to travel long distance for conducting his business in a better way.

During one such incident he has visited far off place located at foot hills of Himalaya. His famous frontier manager Was there with him. Chayan was looking too simple in his loin clothes. On the other hand, frontier manager was looking like a prince, a well dressed one. During one of their visit to a local market of Kashmir, Chayan Vyapari identified a diamond kept in a shop, which was visible even from the other side of road. It was on sale. Chayan deputed his manager to enquire about the precious diamond.

"My master wants to know the cost of the diamond which is visible even from other side of this road." Frontier manager approached the shopkeeper.

After a little pause, shopkeeper asked, "By the way, where's your master?"

"He is there by the side of a tree. He is taking his breakfast and told me to enquire about the diamond that you kept on display for sale."

"Actually, the cost is too much."

"Ok!" There was no scope of further argument. The shopkeeper wanted to guess the potential of Chayan Vyapari just by looking upon his appearances and dress.

The kind of reply admitted by the shopkeeper made Vyapari unhappy. He has decided to go for the deal himself.

"Please count the money you need for the diamond and give it to me." Vyapari placed his bag full of Gold Coins on the table of the shopkeeper.

"It's your fault my elder bother." The shopkeeper admitted his fault of not being capable of identifying a famous merchant moving fearlessly in streets like an ordinary farmer.

"My fault!"

"Yes. Please maintain your dress at least up to a minimum standard."

"Simple living is my family tradition. You please stop identifying people and their capabilities only by looking upon dress."

Finally the diamond of desired type was in the hand of Vyapari. There kept another small diamond. The second one was in the form of a gift. It can keep the memories of their meeting alive forever.

Trying Days

The Tree of Prosperity started growing with adequate pace just after receiving traces of sunlight. Prolonged winter was over.

It made Kameliya more happy.

Grandpa said one cannot force a plant to grow. We can help it to grow by providing manures, water. We can also keep it at a place where it must receive adequate light.

Ultimately the sun is the only source of light for us. She can remember the earlier days. The seed came up with a tender growth. Within few days it started spreading seed leaves. The tender growth was so soft that any gentle touch was also harmful for it. Kameliya was much eager to touch it. Just after returning back from he school, she used to rush to the garden, the place where the plant was trying its best to grow up.

Grandpa told her not to touch the seed leaves of the plant.

Restless Kameliya accepted the words of her Grandpa. Her school days got a new routine. It was in the form of a regular visit to the adjoining garden to take a look upon the growth of the plant.

She came to know about the way plants make their own food. They have greenish pigments in their leaves. They can trap sunlight. They are also helpful in making food for other animals.

After the festival days, the sky changed its nature. Kameliya came to know about the incoming dark days. It was at the coastlines. The sees were also not giving good signals.

All inmates became worried about school vans, shopping and many other daily things. Grandpa was worried about his vegetable garden.

Only Kameliya started expressing her worries about the newly developing sapling. Rest of the other saplings were also located side by side. Rains washed away manures. It has also drained away top covering. The only person helpful was Grandpa. He had all his efforts for protecting the sapling went on.

"Where's the plant!", Kameliya broke her silence after a gap of couple of minutes after watching the meshed up garden of Grandpa.

"Here's the plant. Come in and see.", Grandpa called Kameliya inside his workshop.

The sapling was quite protected in an earthen pot.

Drop of tears, which was waiting in the eyes of Kameliya, got its way out.

It was a happiness. She left her plan of taking snacks and milk in the evening.

"Should I stay with you here, Grandpa?", the appeal of Kameliya was unavoidable for Grandpa. He had no answer for it. It was the time of taking snacks.

From the very next day Kameliya can watch the plant throughout the day. She can go through it after recovering from fever. Family doctor suggested a bed rest for her. These days the plant will be at the intensive care. The plant has also lost its one of the seed leaf. It can struggle with the help of only one food bank.

Trying days for both Kameliya and plant made entire family unhappy.

"Not to give up, is the only thing we can do", these words of Grandpa was an ease for the beloved girl of the family.

"How is the sapling, Grandpa?", Kameliya wanted to know.

"I'm taking care. Don't worry." It was the only thing than the old man can provide Kameliya.

All the three rainy days passed away. Lot of precious things drained away by the violent wind. Kameliya remained inside the room because of her ill-health.

Sunny days, again, made the garden fit for the revival of greenery. The sapling of Kaemliya started regaining its lost vitality. It came out of the earthe pot. It had a new place beside the main building. It was the place where sunlight enters throughout the year.

Kameliya got the permission of the family doctor for opening her window. She has decided to feel the fresh wind and fresh sunlight. The freshness of both the type made her unhappy because of the pale colour of her favourite sapling. Her happiness turned into pale feelings. Her worries about the chances of the survival of the baby plant made her more unhappy.

Sunny days again made the garden fit for the revival of greenery. The sapling of Kaemliya started regaining its lost vitality. It came out of the earthe pot. It had a new place beside the main building. It was the place where sunlight enters throughout the year.

Kameliya got the permission of the family doctor for opening her window. She has decided to feel the fresh wind and fresh sunlight.

The freshness of both the type made her unhappy because of the pale colour of her favourite sapling. Her happiness turned into pale feelings. Her worries about the chances of the survival of the baby plant made her more unhappy.

Days of misery went on for a couple of weeks. Kameliya prepared for joining her school. Exam days were approaching. Before moving to school, she wanted to see the baby plant.

Traces of green buds, newly advancing twig, manuring made by Grandpa and some other small things made Kameliya happy. It was a happiness of full potential. She made her mind for the forthcoming examination.

[1] Hindi term Katha means Stories. Saint Vinoba Bhave translated Shri Madbhagvadgita in Marathi and also wrote a series of books to explain teachings of Gita through simple stories which were also contextually relevant.

[2] Both Ultraviolet and Infrared Radiations are the parts of the invisible band of spectrum incorporated in the Solar Radiation. Our visual sense organ can feel the presence of only visible spectrum comprising seven different colours.

[3] Desire is a state of mind that gives birth to a strong feeling to have something in acquisition or an affinity of wanting something to happen.

For example: I desire only to be left in the state of peaceful mind. Desire cannot kill any intellect, but in a long run, it can suppress the chances of a shift of mind towards something innovative.

[4] Madhavdasji |(1798-1921) was from Bengal and later on entered Vaishnavism. He learned a lot to acquire all sorts of knowledge on Hathayoga duly proposed and framed earlier by Saint Patanjali.

[5]. A Trophic livel signifies the food habit of organisms during their representation as they exhibit in a food chain. Green Plants, for example prepares their own food with the help of sunlight and secures the first position in a food chain and basic position in the food pyramid. Second trophic level is occupied by herbivores, followed by carnivores at the third.

[6] . Saint Aurovindo compiled his works on Yoga and coined it as Integral Yoga because of accommodation of different Yoga Philosophy inside rituals and cultural observations of a community.

[7] . Saint Patanjali was from the Vedic Civilisation who proposed the balanced life process through pracxtiicng Ashtanga Yoga (Eight fold Yoga) in a regular succession for gaining the enlightenment of oneself and for identifying the Aim in life.

[8] . Sabari was a Tribal Woman who offered fruits to Rama and LAxmana during their progression through the forest. She wanted to know about different types of devotion that a follower can follow through for individual ascent in the path of daily life.

[9] . Invation of Kalinga (361 B.C.) by Ashoka was basically for the purpose of finding out the culprit who attacked on his mother and killed her. Historians may possess difference of opinion regarding the main reason of such mass killing that generals of emperor Ashoka materialised in Kalinga. Some locally developed thematic plays confers the possible reasons of killing his brothers before accepting the charge of Magadh.

[10] Dhana Nanda was the last Emperor of Nanda dynasty. Chanakya, the Economic Advisor of Nanda Dynasty, was badly insulted by Dhana Nanda. Also oppression of Dhana Nanda became unbearable. He was not concerned about the problems faced by farmers and artisans of that territory.

[11] . In later period of history name of Chanakya became popular because of his contribution in the field of Economy by developing a balanced Economic Policy for a State (Arthashastra of Koutilya).